BUILDING WORDS

Because you hear it spoken all day and see it in print everywhere, you probably take English for granted. It just IS, like air and water, ever present and never changing. But have you noticed that almost everything changes? Sometimes, change seems to be the only constant! Clothing and hair styles, country landscapes, automobile models, computer technology - always changing. The same goes for the language you speak and take for granted. Over time, words come and go as they are needed, pronunciations change, definitions change, spellings change. Think about how many words you use that you never hear your parents use. Some of those words will be in future dictionaries, so you are yourself responsible for some of the changes we are referring to.

This program focuses on how words are built. The building blocks of words are actually pieces of meaning. The goal of the program is that you will never see an unfamiliar word again without asking yourself what is actually familiar about it. Here is a formula to keep in mind:

Word = prefix(es) + root + suffix(es)

The parentheses are to show that those parts are optional. All every word really needs is a **root**. <u>The root is the core meaning of a word</u>. Figuring out the meanings of words is like solving a problem. In solving this problem, first find the root of the word. Sometimes the root is a word by itself, but most roots must have a prefix or suffix added to them to make words. Either way, the root of a word will be its core meaning. Prefixes and suffixes also have meaning. To figure out what a word means, look for any part whose meaning is familiar. When the meanings of these parts are added together, the underlying meaning of the word will begin to appear.

If the root of the word is its core meaning, what do prefixes and suffixes do?

Prefixes are meaningful pieces that add onto the *front* of roots; they don't change what the root means, but they add information to build words. Sometimes a prefix can actually make a word whose meaning is the opposite of the meaning of the root. This is a little like putting a minus sign in front of a number to turn it into a negative number. So, if you add the prefix *dis-* (which means "not") to the root *agree*, what do you get? The prefix *dis* + the root *agree* = the word *disagree,* meaning "not to agree," the opposite of *to agree*.

Amazingly, if you learn a mere three prefixes, you will be able to know part of the meaning of more than half of all the words in English that have a prefix. Trust us, as you go through the activities in this book, you will learn these three prefixes and many more. In fact, if you look to your left you will see a listing of 67 different prefixes that you will probably run into during the next few years. Sometimes these prefixes are spelled a little differently to make them easier to pronounce when they are added to the root. (For example, when *in* is put onto the front of *legal*, it becomes *il-* instead of *in-*. Think how weird it would be to say *inlegal*.)

　　　　　　　　www.dynamicliteracy.com

What about **Suffixes**? They, too, have meaning. The result is a word that combines the meaning of the suffix with the meaning of the root. For example, the suffix *–less* ("without") + the root *hope* = *hopeless,* ("without expectation.") The root **act** can be used as a verb or as a noun. As a verb, *act* usually refers to the idea of behaving, as in *I always act nice around my parents.* But think about how you might use the following words, all of them *act* + suffix:

acts   My brother acts nice, too.

acting My dog has been acting strange lately.

acted   When he was sick last year, he acted this way.

See how suffixes work? And they work on many, many roots to do exactly what you see them doing here to the root *act.*

The inside of the back cover of this book lists 97 suffixes and what they do to roots. Just like **prefixes**, a few of these **suffixes** are used a whole lot of the time. These and many of the others will be covered in the exercises in this book.

There is an index of the roots included in this book on the back cover. Notice that most of them have more than one spelling. These differences occur for several reasons, but mostly to make words easier to pronounce. We call these groups of spellings a **meaning family**.

A page you will see each week is called "**My Word Wall**", and the first example is on page 8. One thing that makes this program different from other ways to learn vocabulary is that <u>your teacher doesn't give you lists of words</u>. You give them to your teacher! Along with the activities in this book and other parts of the program, use the **My Word Wall** pages to build your own dictionary. You will be amazed by how many words you have by the end of the year.

Have fun with this program! It is all about playing with words.

www.dynamicliteracy.com

Root Squares

How many words can you make?

Start in any square. Your goal is to combine two or more word parts to make as many words in the 'form' family as you can. Write each word and a definition you can think of for it in the space provided at the bottom of the page.

ul	mal	ize
ity	form	ist
con	al	a

_____

_____

_____

_____

_____

_____

_____

_____

_____

Magic Squares

Select the best answer for each of the words in the 'form' family from the numbered definitions. Put the number in the proper space in the Magic Square box. If the total of the numbers is the same both across and down, you have found the magic number!

'form' means shape, appearance, or arrangement

WORDS	DEFINITIONS
A. conformists	1. things that give shape or arrangement to
B. informality	2. quality of not having accepted arrangement
C. transformer	3. shaping or arranging; putting into a reusable pattern or structure
D. oviform	4. shaped like an egg
E. malforming	5. conditions of having one shape or appearance
F. formulated	6. causing to be shaped badly
G. uniformities	7. a device that moves across to another shape
H. conformity	8. reduced to a small arrangement of steps or parts
I. formatting	9. people who easily adapt to a shape or arrangement; people who prefer to comply
	10. similarity or agreement in shape or arrangement; quality of complying

Magic Square Box

A.	B.	C.
D.	E.	F.
G.	H.	I.

Magic Number _____

www.dynamicliteracy.com

4

Stair Steps

Fill in the missing letters of each FORM word by using the definitions below.
FORM means shape, appearance, or arrangement

1. | | | f | o | r | m |
2. | f | o | r | m | | |
3. | | f | o | r | m | |
4. | f | o | r | m | |
5. | f | o | r | m | |
6. | | f | o | r | m |
7. | | | f | o | r | m |
8. | | f | o | r | m |
9. | | | | | f | o | r | m |

1. to give another shape or appearance to; arrange again; to make over or improve
2. a little shape or arrangement; logical arrangement of steps in a process
3. a person giving shape or arrangement to again
4. to reduce to a small arrangement of steps or parts
5. put into accepted arrangement or shape
6. in a manner giving shape to ideas
7. bad shape or structure
8. in a manner serving to provide shape to data
9. acts of moving across to other shapes

The Strange Case of Dr. Jekyll and Mr. Hyde

The good Dr. Jekyll <u>reduces to a small arrangement of parts</u> the idea that people have a good side and a bad side. He develops a liquid potion that he believes will isolate the two <u>shapes or arrangements</u> of the human mind. Without <u>giving shape to his idea</u> to anyone, he drinks the <u>liquid with a specifically arranged recipe</u>. He quickly <u>turns ruined and contorted</u> into an evil being called Mr. Hyde and slinks through the streets committing crimes. He had always been a mannerly <u>person who complied with common appearances</u>, behaving <u>so as to accord with accepted arrangement</u> and properly, but under the influence of the potion, his notion of goodness had <u>become badly shaped</u>. He is aware of his <u>qualities of being ruined and contorted</u> but cannot <u>put into accepted shape</u> the right anti-potion and finally dies as a hated, hunted monster of a human.

<u>Fill in the blanks using words from the **form** family.</u>

1. Dr. Jekyll _____ an idea that people have a split personality.

2. Some people believe that forces of good and evil make up the two _____ of the human mind.

3. The good doctor, without _____ anyone, drank his discovered potion.

4. The _____ that he drank changed his personality.

5. As his personality changes, his body _____ as well.

6. Before, Dr. Jekyll had always been a proper _____ .

7. In public, the doctor had always behaved very _____ .

8. His _____ body reflected the bad change in his character.

9. He was horrified to be aware of the _____ that had overtaken him.

10. Mr. Hyde could not _____ the correct antidote to return to being Dr. Jekyll.

<u>Word Bank</u>

conformist	formalize	formula	malformed
deformities	formally	formulates	transformer
deforms	forms	informing	uniformed
formal	formulaic	informingly	uniformity

www.dynamicliteracy.com

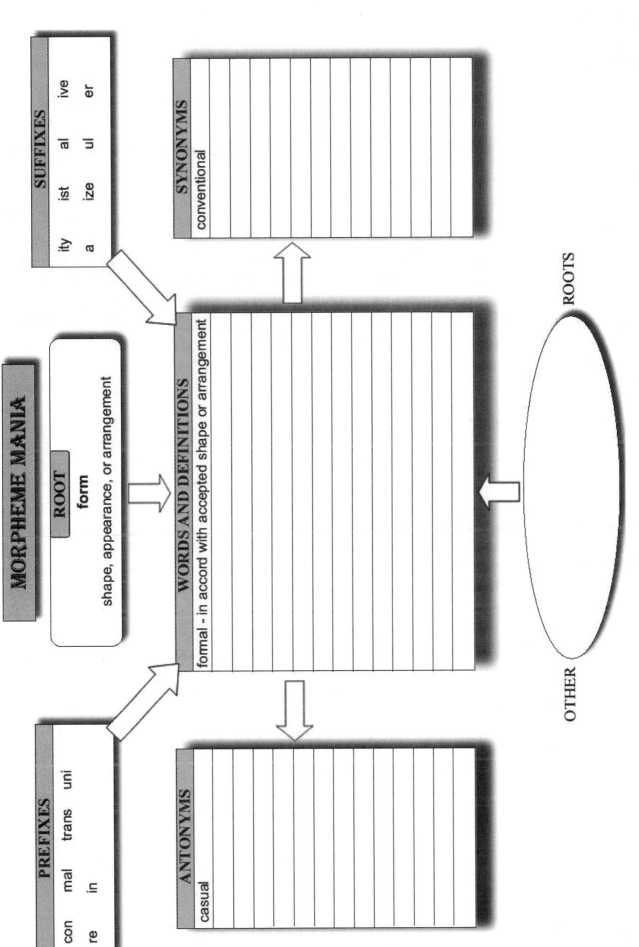

MORPHEME MANIA

PREFIXES

con	mal	uni
re	trans	in

ROOT

form

shape, appearance, or arrangement

SUFFIXES

ity	ist	al	ive
	a	ize	ul	er

WORDS AND DEFINITIONS

formal - in accord with accepted shape or arrangement

SYNONYMS

conventional

ANTONYMS

casual

ROOTS

OTHER

Build as many words as you can for this root family. Use the prefixes and suffixes listed, or add your own. If you use any "combining roots", add them to the "Other Roots" box. Try to think of an antonym and a synonym for each word you build.

Root: *form*

Word	Synonym / Antonym	Word	Synonym / Antonym

Morphemes for this meaning family

Prefixes	Roots	Suffixes

Root Squares

How many words can you make?

Start in any square. Your goal is to combine two or more word parts to make as many words in the 'pon, pone, pos, pose, post' family as you can. Write each word and a definition you can think of for it in the space provided at the bottom of the page.

ful	it	ly
pur	pon, pone, pos, pose, post	sup
ive	ex	ure

_____

_____

_____

_____

_____

_____

_____

_____

www.dynamicliteracy.com

Magic Squares

Select the best answer for each of the words in the 'pon, pone, pos, pose, post' family from the numbered definitions. Put the number in the proper space in the Magic Square box. If the total of the numbers is the same both across and down, you have found the magic number!

'pon, pone, pos, pose, post' means to place, to put

WORDS	DEFINITIONS
A. components	1. places oneself back; rests
B. composing	2. act or process of putting away; the right to throw away or use
C. disposal	3. put down on top of something
D. depositing	4. putting down; putting money into a bank for safekeeping
E. exponent	5. put off until afterwards
F. opponents	6. people who are placed against; rivals, as in games
G. postponed	7. putting together; creating, especially music or poetry
H. superimposed	8. something put outside; a math symbol denoting numerical power
I. predispositions	9. items put together; units that make a whole
	10. acts of being put aside beforehand; tendencies

Magic Square Box

A.	B.	C.
D.	**E.**	**F.**
G.	**H.**	**I.**

Magic Number ____

www.dynamicliteracy.com

Fill in the missing letters of each PON, PONE, POS, POSE, POST word
by using the definitions below.
PON, PONE, POS, POSE, POST means to place, to put

1.			p	o	s								
2.			p	o	s								
3.				p	o	s	e						
4.			p	o	s								
5.						p	o	s	e				
6.				p	o	s	e						
7.				p	o	s								
8.						p	o	s					

1. placed oneself back; rested
2. act of being put out; act of being publicly shown
3. in a manner put forth; for a specific reason
4. placement in conflict against
5. to put down on top of something
6. in a manner characteristic of things put forth; in a manner having many reasons
7. in a manner related to being placed outside; so as to relate to numerical power
8. related to being placed in front; pertaining to being put before an object
9. act of being put aside beforehand; a tendency

11

Inge and Quentin decided to take a <u>place or stand</u> to start conserving. They encouraged their friends to make a commitment <u>characteristic of things set forth</u> to saving energy and resources and to make a <u>suggestion offered</u> to their families to help. They explained how to build a pile <u>of organic material put together</u> in which they <u>put down</u> raked leaves, yard clippings, and organic garbage. After the waste <u>stops being put together</u>, it becomes beneficial mulch for flower and vegetable gardens. Inge and Quentin persuaded some people who had been <u>likely to put up argument against</u> that they could save money and have fun, too.

They <u>put forth</u> a recycling project in the school cafeteria. They did some research and presented an <u>act of showing in public</u> about non-recyclable trays and utensils. Inge and Quentin were an influence <u>put firmly and well</u> on the other students and adults at their school.

<u>Fill in the blanks using words from the **pon, pone, pos, pose, post** family.</u>

1. Inge and Quentin decided to take up a _____ for conservation.

2. Some of Inge's and Quentin's friends made a _____ commitment to join them.

3. Some students made _____ to their families to join in on the plan.

4. A _____ pile is a source of good mulch for gardens.

5. Waste that is _____ there breaks down or _____.

6. People who had been _____ to conservation were persuaded by the money-saving aspect.

7. The students _____ a recycling project in the cafeteria.

8. After some research, they gave an _____ about non-recyclable items.

9. Quentin and Inge were a _____ influence on other students and adults as well.

Word Bank

compost	deposited	opposed	positive	proposition
composted	exposition	opposition	proposals	purposeful
decomposes	impose	position	proposed	suppositional

www.dynamicliteracy.com

MORPHEME MANIA

PREFIXES
re
ex   dis   sup
pur

ROOT
pon, pone, pos, pose, post
to place or put

SUFFIXES
ion   it   ful   ive
ly   ure   ent   ial

WORDS AND DEFINITIONS
suppose - to put up; to offer as a suggestion

SYNONYMS
brainstorm

ANTONYMS
know

ROOTS

OTHER

Build as many words as you can for this root family. Use the prefixes and suffixes listed, or add your own. If you use any "combining roots", add them to the "Other Roots" box. Try to think of an antonym and a synonym for each word you build.

www.DynamicLiteracy.com

My Word Wall

Name _____

Root: *pon, pone, pos, pose, post*

Word	Synonym / Antonym	Word	Synonym / Antonym

Morphemes for this meaning family

Prefixes	Roots	Suffixes

Root Squares

How many words can you make?

Start in any square. Your goal is to combine two or more word parts to make as many words in the 'voc, voci, vok, voke' family as you can. Write each word and a definition you can think of for it in the space provided at the bottom of the page.

a	ad	e
ate	voc, voci, vok, voke	in
ive	ion	pro

_____

_____

_____

_____

_____

_____

_____

_____

Magic Squares

Select the best answer for each of the words in the 'voc, voci, vok, voke' family from the numbered definitions. Put the number in the proper space in the Magic Square box. If the total of the numbers is the same both across and down, you have found the magic number!

'voc, voci, vok, voke' means speech; voice, call, say

<u>WORDS</u>

A. advocates
B. equivocating
C. revoked
D. provocative
E. invocation
F. unequivocal
G. vociferous
H. vocation
I. vocal

<u>DEFINITIONS</u>

1. tending to call forth to action
2. that which calls a person away; an enjoyed activity other than a person's job
3. a calling together for a meeting or ceremony
4. related to the voice; said aloud
5. called back; canceled
6. job to which a person is called
7. speaking for balanced different viewpoints; avoiding a direct answer
8. the act of calling upon; the act of summoning a higher power for help
9. speaks to; supports an iss
10. related to the job to which a person is called
11. tending to loud speech that carries far
12. not calling on balanced sides of an issue; without doubt or ambiguity

Magic Square Box

A.	B.	C.
D.	E.	F.
G.	H.	I.

Magic Number _____

www.dynamicliteracy.com

Stair Steps

Fill in the missing letters of each VOC, VOCI, VOL, VOKE word
by using the definitions below.

VOC, VOCI, VOK, VOKE means speech; voice, call, say

1.			v	o	k	e						
2.			v	o	k	e						
3.			v	o	c							
4.	v	o	c									
5.		v	o	c								
6.	v	o	c	i								
7.			v	o	c							
8.			v	o	c							
9.			v	o	c							

1. to call back; to cancel
2. calls upon; summons a higher power for help
3. to speak to; to support an issue
4. to speak or sing
5. tending to call forth or out; likely to summon a memory or mood
6. tending to loud speech that carries far
7. a calling together for a meeting or ceremony
8. speaking for balanced different viewpoints; avoiding a direct answer
9. in a manner calling forth to action

www.dynamicliteracy.com

Gettysburg Address

In 1863, President Abraham Lincoln stood at a podium in Gettysburg, Pennsylvania, to speak to an idea about the future of the United States. Instead of speaking in a manner to call forth action, Lincoln spoke his view in a way that called out memories of the spirit of the American Revolution, which had ended just 87 years earlier. His speech called upon the principles of human equality set forth in the Declaration of Independence. He did not balance words when he stated his desire for a government "of the people, by the people, and for the people." President Lincoln was not the featured speaker that day. That honor belonged to Edward Everett, who had served as Secretary of State, U.S. Senator, U.S. Representative, Governor of Massachusetts, and President of Harvard, and he was considered the greatest speaker of the day. After the calling together by Reverend T.H. Stockton, Everett spoke for two hours. Then President Lincoln spoke for two minutes. Lincoln did not wish to call forth more division in the country but to stress the right that cannot be called back or canceled of people to live as equals. His brief address is one of the most famous speeches in world history. Has anyone ever heard of Everett's long speech?

Fill in the blanks using words from the **voc, voci, vok, voke** family.

1. President Lincoln hoped to _____ to the audience his idea of America.

2. The President did not speak _____ as if to stir up the crowd.

3. Lincoln _____ his powerful view in just a few sentences.

4. The address which he gave _____ memories of America's purpose.

5. His words _____ the principles of human equality.

6. He did not _____ about the idea that in America, the government is of, by, and for all the people.

7. The featured speaker was considered the greatest _____ of that time.

8. Before the speech, there was a _____ calling the people together.

9. Lincoln did not want to _____ either hatred or a victory celebration.

10. Lincoln felt that rights given in the Declaration of Independence were _____.

Word Bank

advocate	evoked	provocatively	vocalized
convocation	invoked	provoke	vocalizer
equivocate	irrevocable	revoking	vocation

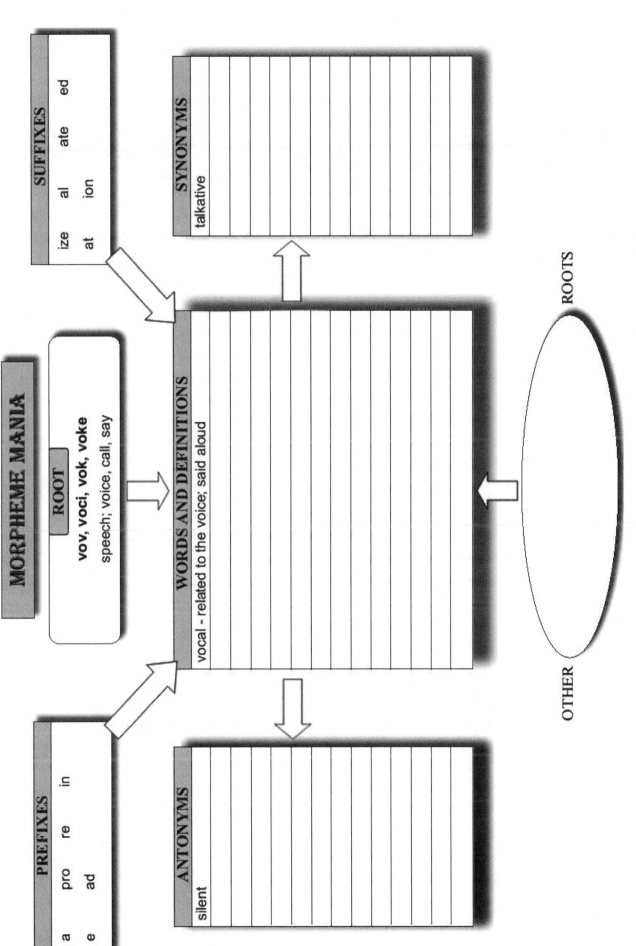

MORPHEME MANIA

PREFIXES

a
pro   re   in
e
ad

ROOT

vov, voci, vok, voke
speech; voice, call, say

SUFFIXES

ize
al   ate   ed
at
ion

WORDS AND DEFINITIONS

vocal - related to the voice; said aloud

SYNONYMS

talkative

ANTONYMS

silent

OTHER ROOTS

Build as many words as you can for this root family. Use the prefixes and suffixes listed, or add your own. If you use any "combining roots", add them to the "Other Roots" box. Try to think of an antonym and a synonym for each word you build.

www.DynamicLiteracy.com

Root: *voc, voci, vok, voke*

Word	Synonym / Antonym	Word	Synonym / Antonym

Morphemes for this meaning family

Prefixes	Roots	Suffixes

Root Squares

How many words can you make?

Start in any square. Your goal is to combine two or more word parts to make as many words in the 'grat, grate, grati, grac, grace' family as you can. Write each word and a definition you can think of for it in the space provided at the bottom of the page.

fic	ate	ful
con	grat, grate, grati, grac, grace	ious
ul	ion	dis

_____

_____

_____

_____

_____

_____

_____

_____

www.dynamicliteracy.com

Magic Squares

Select the best answer for each of the words in the 'grat, grate, grati, grac, grace' family from the numbered definitions. Put the number in the proper space in the Magic Square box. If the total of the numbers is the same both across and down, you have found the magic number!

grat, grate, grati, grac, grace ' means agreeable, thankful, pleasing

WORDS	DEFINITIONS
A. congratulate	1. serving to express pleasure with; relating to praise of another's accomplishment
B. disgraceful	2. to express pleasure with; to give praise for another's accomplishment
C. grace	3. not pleasing in form or action; nor refined or elegant
D. gracefully	4. a person who is not thankful
E. ingrate	5. trying to make oneself agreeable to another person
F. gratuitous	6. in a pleasing manner; in a refined and elegant manner
G. gratefully	7. a pleasing and agreeable quality; a prayer of thanks
H. ingratiating	8. done only for thanks; free
I. ungraceful	9. marked by an unpleasing quality; shameful
	10. in a manner full of thanks; in an appreciative manner

Magic Square Box

A.	B.	C.
D.	E.	F.
G.	H.	I.

Magic Number ____

Stair Steps

Fill in the missing letters of each GRAT, GRATE, GRATI, GRAC, GRACE word
by using the definitions below.

GRAT, GRATE, GRATI, GRAC, GRACE means agreeable, thankful, pleasing

1. **g r a t i** _ _ _
2. **g r a c e** _ _ _
3. _ _ **g r a c** _ _
4. **g r a t** _ _ _ _
5. _ **g r a t i** _ _
6. _ **g r a t i** _ _
7. _ **g r a c e** _ _
8. **g r a t i** _ _ _ _ _
9. _ _ **g r a t** _ _ _ _ _

1. to please or make thankful; to fulfill satisfyingly
2. pleasing in form or action; refined and elegant
3. made unpleasing or unagreeable; shamed
4. expressions of thanks for service; tips
5. not pleased or satisfied
6. trying to make oneself agreeable to another person
7. in a manner marked by an unpleasant quality; shamefully
8. acts of being made pleased; satisfied fulfillments
9. expressions of pleasure with; praises for another's accomplishment

23

A Wedding Party Ruined

Everyone was <u>expressing pleasure and praise</u> to Peleus and Thetis at their wedding party. Thetis, a nymph <u>pleasing in form and action</u>, was <u>in a pleasing and agreeable manner</u> receiving gifts from all the gods and goddesses. The deities wanted to <u>fulfill completely</u> the couple's every need. Peleus and Thetis were <u>full of thanks</u> for the splendid company that was bringing <u>pleasure and favor to</u> their wedding and for the excellent gifts <u>serving to bring pleasure and favor</u> that they were receiving.

One goddess, Discord, had not been invited, but she had the <u>quality of lacking pleasing social behavior</u> to attend anyway. She also offered a gift that brought <u>a loss of pleasing quality</u> to the wedding party. That gift, a golden apple thrown among the guests, caused a quarrel that would lead eventually to the Trojan War, <u>marked with shame and unpleasantness</u>.

<u>Fill in the blanks using words from the **grat, grate, grati, grac, grace** family</u>.

1. Everyone was _____ the happy couple on their special day.

2. The bride was a beautiful and _____ nymph.

3. Gifts were being received _____ from the gods and goddesses.

4. The gods and goddesses wanted to _____ all the couple's needs.

5. In return, Peleus and Thetis were _____ for the company and the gifts.

6. Wondrous guests were _____ the wedding party on this occasion.

7. Their excellent _____ gifts made the couple very happy.

8. Discord had the _____ to show up uninvited.

9. Discord also presented a gift that brought _____ to this wedding party.

10. That gift led to the long and _____ Trojan War.

<u>Word Bank</u>

congratulating	disgraceful	graciously	gratuity
congratulatory	graceful	grateful	ingrate
disgrace	gracing	gratify	ungraciousness

MORPHEME MANIA

PREFIXES

dis   con   un

SUFFIXES

ful   ul   ious   ed
ate   ion

ROOT

grat, grate, grati, grac, grace
agreeable, thankful, pleasing

WORDS AND DEFINITIONS

ungrateful – not properly thankful

SYNONYMS

unthankful

ANTONYMS

appreciative

ROOTS

fic – to make or do

OTHER

Build as many words as you can for this root family. Use the prefixes and suffixes listed, or add your own. If you use any "combining roots", add them to the "Other Roots" box. Try to think of an antonym and a synonym for each word you build.

Root: *grat, grate, grati, grac, grace*

Word	Synonym / Antonym	Word	Synonym / Antonym

Morphemes for this meaning family

Prefixes	Roots	Suffixes

Root Squares

How many words can you make?

Start in any square. Your goal is to combine two or more word parts to make as many words in the 'gest' family as you can. Write each word and a definition you can think of for it in the space provided at the bottom of the page.

di	ion	ant
ive	gest	ible
sug	ure	con

_____

_____

_____

_____

_____

_____

_____

_____

www.dynamicliteracy.com

Magic Squares

Select the best answer for each of the words in the 'gest' family from the numbered definitions. Put the number in the proper space in the Magic Square box. If the total of the numbers is the same both across and down, you have found the magic number!

'gest' means to take, bring, or carry

WORDS
A. congested
B. decongestants
C. digested
D. gestured
E. indigestible
F. suggests
G. gesturing
H. decongest
I. digest

DEFINITIONS
1. brought an idea forth; conveyed meaning by a body movement
2. tending to bring together; tending to clog
3. process of carrying to full development; period of maturing
4. to take tightly bound matter apart
5. substances that untighten matter brought together; medicines that help unclog
6. to take apart into smaller units; to metabolize or assimilate into the body
7. took apart into smaller units; metabolized or assimilated into the body
8. brings up; proposes an idea
9. brought together; clogged
10. act of carrying on or performing; act of expressing with body motion
11. bringing an idea forth; conveying meaning by a body movement
12. inability to be taken apart into smaller units; not able to be metabolized or assimilated into the body

Magic Square Box

A.	B.	C.
D.	E.	F.
G.	H.	I.

Magic Number _____

www.dynamicliteracy.com

Stair Steps

Fill in the missing letters of each GEST word
by using the definitions below.
GEST means to take, bring, or carry

1.			g	e	s	t							
2.			g	e	s	t							
3.	g	e	s	t									
4.			g	e	s	t							
5.			g	e	s	t							
6.				g	e	s	t						
7.	g	e	s	t									
8.				g	e	s	t						
9.	g	e	s	t									

1. to take apart into smaller units; to metabolize or assimilate into the body
2. takes apart into smaller units; metabolizes or assimilates into the body
3. brought an idea forth; conveyed meaning by a body movement
4. brought together; clogged
5. tending to bring up; tending to propose an idea
6. act or process of not taking apart into smaller units; difficulty metabolizing or assimilating into the body
7. carried on or performed; expressed with body motion
8. substances that untighten matter brought together; medicines that help unclog
9. acts of carrying on or performing; acts of expressing with body motions

29

Too Much Congestion!

The traffic is so <u>clogged</u> on the main road that Abby can rarely enter onto it from her street. She <u>brought up an idea</u> to the highway department that they extend bus service or put up a stop light, but nothing was done about her <u>proposals</u>. Even the stop sign farther up the road did nothing to <u>unclog</u> the traffic, since so many people ran the sign anyway. It was enough to give Abby <u>difficulty assimilating her food</u> every morning.   One day, as traffic never let up, Abby was thinking about the article she had read in an auto club's <u>magazine that gives summaries</u> called Traffic Misery.   The article was <u>bringing up an idea</u> that most people lose all sense of manners and respect when they are driving, and that <u>the act of clogging</u> makes people nasty.   One particularly bad morning, Abby was beginning to believe it when finally one nice motorist slowed a bit and thoughtfully <u>conveyed meaning with hand motion</u> for her to pull out safely onto the road in front of him.

<u>Fill in the blanks using words from the **gest** family.</u>

1. Abby can't get off her street onto the main road because traffic is so _____.

2. She has _____ some solutions that would help cut down the traffic.

3. Her _____ were met with no action taken.

4. Stop signs could help to _____ traffic flow, but many people do not obey them.

5. Upset at the behavior of so many drivers, Abby nearly gets _____.

6. An auto club _____ recently published an article on traffic misery.

7. The article was _____ that driving makes people less mannerly.

8. One morning the road _____ was even worse than usual.

9. Finally a kind motorist _____ for Abby to enter the road in front of him.

Word Bank

congested	digest	gestured	suggesting
congestion	gestation	indigestion	suggestions
decongest	gesticulations	suggested	suggestively

www.dynamicliteracy.com

MORPHEME MANIA

PREFIXES

con	di	in	de
sug			

ROOT

gest

to take, bring, or carry

SUFFIXES

ible	ant	ure	ion
ive	ed		

WORDS AND DEFINITIONS

suggest - to bring up an idea

SYNONYMS

recommend

ANTONYMS

conceal

ROOTS

OTHER

Build as many words as you can for this root family. Use the prefixes and suffixes listed, or add your own. If you use any "combining roots", add them to the "Other Roots" box. Try to think of an antonym and a synonym for each word you build.

www.DynamicLiteracy.com

My Word Wall

Root: *gest*

Word	Synonym / Antonym	Word	Synonym / Antonym

Morphemes for this meaning family

Prefixes	Roots	Suffixes

Root Squares

How many words can you make?

Start in any square. Your goal is to combine two or more word parts to make as many words in the 'soci, socio' family as you can. Write each word and a definition you can think of for it in the space provided at the bottom of the page.

as	anti	ity
abil	soci, socio	al
dis	ism	ate

_____

_____

_____

_____

_____

_____

_____

_____

Magic Squares

Select the best answer for each of the words in the 'soci, socio' family from the numbered definitions. Put the number in the proper space in the Magic Square box. If the total of the numbers is the same both across and down, you have found the magic number!

'soci, socio' means related to others - companions, partners, allies

WORDS	DEFINITIONS
A. antisocial	1. not inclined to relate to others
B. associate	2. shunning companions, partners, and allies; unfriendly
C. disassociate	3. in a manner showing desire for company of others
D. sociology	4. interacting with companions
E. socialist	5. joining as a partner
F. socializing	6. study of people in companionship and alliance
G. sociologist	7. to remove oneself from companions or partners
H. socially	8. a person having a view centered on the needs of others
I. associating	9. to join as a partner; the person who is a partner to
	10. studier of people in companionship and alliance

Magic Square Box

A.	B.	C.
D.	E.	F.
G.	H.	I.

Magic Number ____

www.dynamicliteracy.com

Stair Steps

Fill in the missing letters of each SOCI, SOCIO word
by using the definitions below.
SOCI, SOCIO means related to others—companions, partners, allies

1.	s	o	c	i									
2.	s	o	c	i									
3.	s	o	c	i									
4.			s	o	c	i							
5.	s	o	c	i									
6.	s	o	c	i	o								
7.			s	o	c	i							
8.					s	o	c	i					

1. partners and allies collectively
2. pertaining to partners and allies collectively
3. political view centered on the needs of others
4. joined as a partner; became a partner to
5. people who enjoy interacting with companions
6. studiers of people in companionship and alliance
7. quality of not relating to others
8. act of removing oneself from companions or partners

35 www.dynamicliteracy.com

 Opposites Attract

Studies conducted by <u>people who study companionship and alliance</u> have shown some interesting facts about couples. The data indicate a strong <u>partnership</u> between personality types and length of relationships. In general, couples who are a lot alike don't stay together as long as couples who are quite different from one another. In many successful long-term relationships, one person may be highly <u>preferring to live among others</u> and the other person relatively <u>preferring not to live among others</u>. If you are shy, you may be attracted to a person who is a <u>person who loves companionship</u>, because that is a trait you wish you had more of. On the other hand, two people who are too much alike may <u>make a connection of</u> their own short-comings with their partner. Such behavior often leads to a <u>moving away from a partnership</u> by the couple. Of course if you are <u>opposed to living among others</u>, you probably won't have a relationship with anyone! People who behave <u>in a manner opposed to living among others</u> often find themselves shunned by <u>the collective group of partners and alliances</u>.

<u>Fill in the blanks with words from the **soci**, **socio** family.</u>

1. People who study people in relationships with other people are called _____.

2. There is a strong _____ between types of personalities and personal
    relationships.

3. Some people enjoy being _____ and getting among people frequently.

4. Others are very _____ and prefer not to be among people.

5. A shy person may be attracted to his or her opposite, the party-loving and lively
    _____.

6. If you have a relationship with someone just like you, you might _____ things
    you don't like about yourself with that other person.

7. Sometimes people too much alike undergo a _____ and go their separate ways.

8. People who are completely _____ and don't like people at all will probably not
    begin a relationship.

9. Behaving _____ will cause you to be avoided by _____.

Word Bank

antisocial	association	socialism	sociological
antisocially	disassociation	socialite	sociologists
associate	social	society	unsocial

MORPHEME MANIA

PREFIXES

dis	as	in	anti

ROOT

soci, socio

related to others - companions, partners, allies

SUFFIXES

ism	al	abil	ist
	ate	ity	y

WORDS AND DEFINITIONS

social – living with others

SYNONYMS

neighborly

ANTONYMS

unfriendly

ROOTS

OTHER

log – word, speech, study, reason

Build as many words as you can for this root family. Use the prefixes and suffixes listed, or add your own. If you use any "combining roots", add them to the "Other Roots" box. Try to think of an antonym and a synonym for each word you build.

www.DynamicLiteracy.com

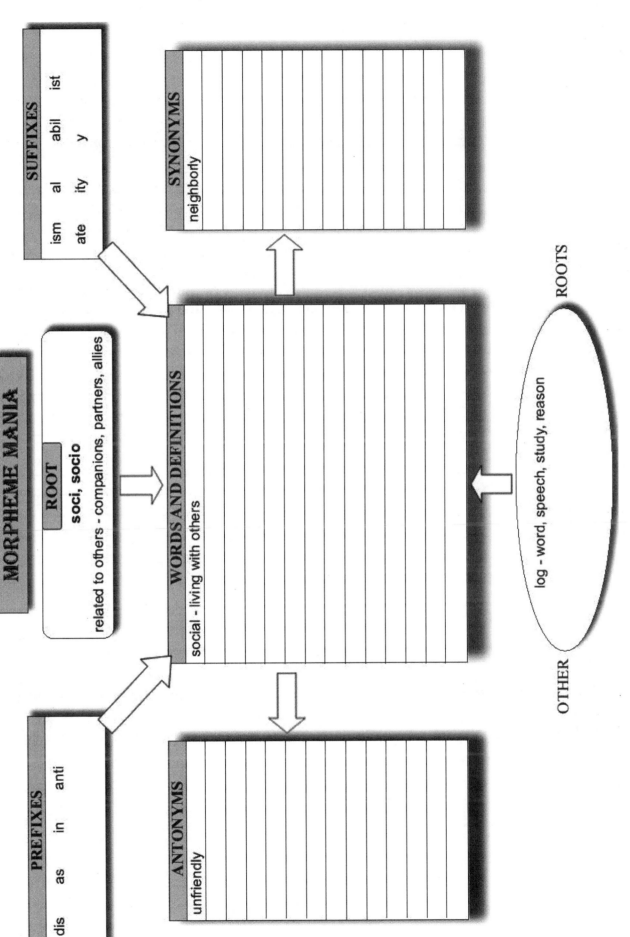

Root: *soci, socio*

Word	Synonym / Antonym	Word	Synonym / Antonym

Morphemes for this meaning family

Prefixes	Roots	Suffixes

Root Squares

How many words can you make?

Start in any square. Your goal is to combine two or more word parts to make as many words in the 'arch, archaeo, archa, arche, archi' family as you can. Write each word and a definition you can think of for it in the space provided at the bottom of the page.

ive	y	tect
ure	arch, archaeo, archa, arche, archi	olig
an	log	ic

_____

_____

_____

_____

_____

_____

_____

_____

Magic Squares

Select the best answer for each of the words in the 'arch, archaeo, archa, arche, archi' family from the numbered definitions. Put the number in the proper space in the Magic Square box. If the total of the numbers is the same both across and down, you have found the magic number!

'arch, archaeo, archa, arche, archi' means early, chief, first, rule

<u>WORDS</u>

A. anarchy
B. archaic
C. archconservative
D. archetypal
E. archliberals
F. matriarch
G. monarchies
H. patriarchal
I. patriarchy

<u>DEFINITIONS</u>

1. chief advocates of unrestricted personal freedom
2. a person who advocates not having rule or government
3. pertaining to original or early records
4. an area ruled by a fatherly figure
5. chief advocate of protecting or keeping as is
6. areas ruled by one person
7. the condition of not having rule or government
8. of an original form by which later ones are judged
9. belonging to an earlier time
10. the chief planner of a building project
11. ruled by a fatherly figure
12. a woman who rules a family or group as a mother

Magic Square Box

A.	B.	C.
D.	E.	F.
G.	H.	I.

Magic Number ____

www.dynamicliteracy.com

Stair Steps

Fill in the missing letters of each ARCH, ARCHAEO, ARCHA, ARCHE, ARCHI word by using the definitions below.

ARCH, ARCHAEO, ARCHA, ARCHE, ARCHI means early, chief, first, rule

#												
1.			a	r	c	h						
2.				a	r	c	h					
3.	a	r	c	h	e							
4.	a	r	c	h								
5.					a	r	c	h				
6.					a	r	c	h				
7.	a	r	c	h	a	e	o					
8.	a	r	c	h	a	e	o					
9.	a	r	c	h	i							

1. the condition of not having rule or government
2. rule by one person
3. original form against which later ones are judged
4. people in charge of caring for early records
5. ruled by a motherly figure
6. areas ruled by fatherly figures
7. a person who studies items from earlier time periods
8. related to the study of items from early times
9. in a manner relating to a chief building design

History Careers

The history of England fascinates Nigel. He would love to be the <u>keeper of records</u> for old documents related to the British <u>rule by one person</u>. The period <u>belonging to an early time</u> before the Romans arrived is especially interesting, and Nigel and his friend Miruna, <u>a person who studies items from early time periods</u>, enjoy visiting Stonehenge. They both also enjoy the historical <u>chief building design</u> of each <u>one-person ruler</u> of England. There is even a style Cromwellian, named for the brief period of the <u>rule by a few</u> after the execution of King Charles I. Nigel and Miruna were surprised to learn that the <u>chief building designer</u> who redesigned London after the Great Fire of 1666 also has a building at an American college named for him. Their favorite style is that of Queen Victoria, the <u>mother-ruler</u> of European royalty.

<u>Fill in the blanks using words from the **arch, archaeo, archa, arche, archi** family.</u>

1. One career that appeals to Nigel is that of _____ for the old documents of England.

2. The British _____ has continued almost unbroken for over 1300 years.

3. The _____ period when Stonehenge was built fascinates Miruna.

4. Miruna is an _____ who studies the ancient artifacts of humans.

5. Many kings and queens have given their names to types of _____.

6. One _____, Charles I, was executed by followers of Cromwell.

7. Cromwell's government was not a monarchy but an _____.

8. The _____ Christopher Wren has a building named for him at the College of William & Mary.

9. Because many of her descendants are nobles throughout Europe, Queen Victoria is called their _____.

<u>Word Bank</u>

archaeologist	archetype	archivist	monarchy
archconservative	architect	matriarch	oligarchy
archaic	architecture	monarch	patriarch

www.dynamicliteracy.com

MORPHEME MANIA

PREFIXES

olig

an   mon

SUFFIXES

ic   y   ure   al

ive   ist

ROOT

arch, archaeo, archa, arche, archi

early, chief, first, rule

WORDS AND DEFINITIONS

archaic – belonging to an earlier time

SYNONYMS

dated

ANTONYMS

modern

ROOTS

log – word, speech, study

tect – art, skill; build

OTHER

Build as many words as you can for this root family. Use the prefixes and suffixes listed, or add your own. If you use any "combining roots", add them to the "Other Roots" box. Try to think of an antonym and a synonym for each word you build.

www.DynamicLiteracy.com

Root: *arch, archaeo, archa, arche, archi*

Word	Synonym / Antonym	Word	Synonym / Antonym

Morphemes for this meaning family

Prefixes	Roots	Suffixes

Root Squares

How many words can you make?

Start in any square. Your goal is to combine two or more word parts to make as many words in the 'ped, pede, pedi, pedo' family as you can. Write each word and a definition you can think of for it in the space provided at the bottom of the page.

ex	centi	ion
ence	ped, pede, pedi, pedo	im
ment	al	ite

_____

_____

_____

_____

_____

_____

_____

_____

Magic Squares

Select the best answer for each of the words in the 'ped, pede, pedi, pedo' family from the numbered definitions. Put the number in the proper space in the Magic Square box. If the total of the numbers is the same both across and down, you have found the magic number!

'ped, pede, pedi, pedo' means foot; leg

WORDS	DEFINITIONS
A. bipeds	1. a creature with "a hundred" legs and feet
B. impede	2. get one's foot in the way; to hinder progress
C. millipede	3. devices for measuring distance covered on foot
D. pedaling	4. four-footed animals
E. pedicures	5. things blocked by foot; hindrances
F. quadrupeds	6. cares and treatments for the feet
G. pedometers	7. animals with two feet
H. pedigrees	8. operating a vehicle by foot
I. impediments	9. a creature with "a thousand" legs and feet
	10. things shaped like a crane's foot; charts of one's ancestors

Magic Square Box

A.	B.	C.
D.	E.	F.
G.	H.	I.

Magic Number ____

www.dynamicliteracy.com

Stair Steps

Fill in the missing letters of each PED, PEDE, PEDI, PEDO word
by using the definitions below.
PED, PEDE, PEDI, PEDO means foot; leg

1.			p	e	d							
2.	p	e	d									
3.	p	e	d	i								
4.	p	e	d	i								
5.						p	e	d	e			
6.			p	e	d	i						
7.			p	e	d	i						
8.			p	e	d							

1. animals with two feet
2. operated a vehicle by foot
3. something shaped like a crane's foot; a chart of one's ancestors
4. cares and treatments for the feet
5. creatures with "a hundred" legs and feet
6. things blocked by foot; hindrances
7. acts of having feet out of the way; acts of straightforward
8. in a manner setting out on foot; in an efficient and unhindered manner

Pet Show Mishap

To raise funds for a trip to the art gallery, the class held a pet show. All the students were excited to show off their pets' talents. One student brought a <u>creature with a hundred legs</u> circus. Another had a dog that could <u>use the feet to power</u> a kiddie car with its back paws on the <u>foot-operated devices</u> and its front paws on the steering wheel. Not one fancy <u>crane-foot-shaped chart</u> could be found among all the entrants. Some had had special <u>foot-treatments</u> done on their claws or a bath with fancy pet shampoo, but they were all just family pets.

There were so many entries that the judges had to <u>remove barriers from</u> the proceedings by placing the contestants into categories and then have the winners of the categories compete in the final show. That was the only <u>blockage</u> to any pet's winning. It had to win its own category.

Once the categories were won, the judges set out to rate the rest <u>in an unhindered manner</u>. Everyone had fun and the only problem occurred when the <u>creatures with a hundred legs</u> escaped from their circus box and headed for freedom.

<u>Fill in the blanks using words from the **ped**, **pede**, **pedi**, **pedo** family.</u>

1. One child brings a _____ circus to the pet show.

2. Another student's dog could _____ a kiddie car.

3. The dog used its back feet on the two _____.

4. A _____ are fancy papers to show a pet's ancestors.

5. Some pets had had _____ done on their claws.

6. To move the proceedings along, the judges had to _____ the judging.

7. Winning its own category was a pet's only _____ to winning the final prize.

8. After judging the categories, the judges rated the rest _____.

9. The _____ presented the only problem of the day by escaping.

<u>Word Bank</u>

centipede	expeditionary	impediment	pedicure
centipedes	expeditiously	pedal	pedicures
expedite	impede	pedals	pedigree
	impeder	pedaling	

www.dynamicliteracy.com

MORPHEME MANIA

PREFIXES
centi	im	ex

SUFFIXES
er	y	ite	ence
ly	ent	ion	

ROOT
ped, pede, pedi, pedo

foot or leg

WORDS AND DEFINITIONS
impede – get one's foot in the way of; hinder

SYNONYMS
block

ANTONYMS
unclog

ROOTS
OTHER

cure – care
gree – crane (the bird)

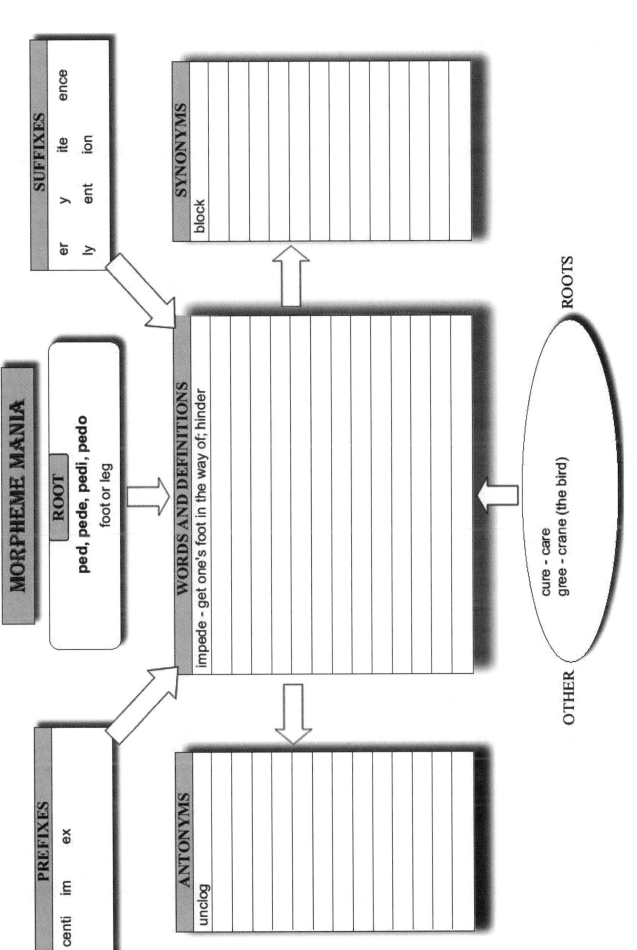

Build as many words as you can for this root family. Use the prefixes and suffixes listed, or add your own. If you use any "combining roots", add them to the "Other Roots" box. Try to think of an antonym and a synonym for each word you build.

www.DynamicLiteracy.com

Root: *ped, pede, pedi, pedo*

Word	Synonym / Antonym	Word	Synonym / Antonym

Morphemes for this meaning family

Prefixes	Roots	Suffixes

Root Squares

How many words can you make?

Start in any square. Your goal is to combine two or more word parts to make as many words in the 'nounc, nounce, nunci' family as you can. Write each word and a definition you can think of for it in the space provided at the bottom of the page.

ion	ate	e
de	nounc, nounce, nunci	pro
re	an	mis

_____

_____

_____

_____

_____

_____

_____

_____

Magic Squares

Select the best answer for each of the words in the 'nounc, nounce, nunci' family from the numbered definitions. Put the number in the proper space in the Magic Square box. If the total of the numbers is the same both across and down, you have found the magic number!

'nounc, nounce, nunci' means report, message; say, speak

WORDS	DEFINITIONS
A. announcement	1. the act of speaking forth; act of declaring formally and clearly
B. announcers	2. to speak down; to condemn a person or thing
C. announcing	3. not able to be spoken forth; not able to be declared formally or clearly
D. enunciate	4. act of speaking down; act of condemning a person or thing
E. pronounceable	5. people who report to; people who state or give notice
F. pronunciation	6. speaks against; gives up or rejects something
G. renounces	7. a message reported to; act of stating or giving notice
H. denunciation	8. to speak out; to speak formally and clearly
I. mispronunciation	9. reporting to; stating or giving notice
	10. speaks forth incorrectly; says a word or name wrong
	11. the speaking forth incorrectly; act of saying a word or name wrong
	12. able to be spoken forth; able to be declared formally or clearly

Magic Square Box

A.	B.	C.
D.	E.	F.
G.	H.	I.

Magic Number _____

www.dynamicliteracy.com

Stair Steps

Fill in the missing letters of each NOUNC, NOUNCE, NUNCI word
by using the definitions below.

NOUNC, NOUNCE, NUNCI means report, message; say, speak

1.			n	o	u	n	c	e				
2.		n	o	u	n	c						
3.			n	o	u	n	c					
4.	n	u	n	c	i							
5.	n	u	n	c	i							
6.	n	o	u	n	c	e						
7.				n	o	u	n	c				
8.				n	o	u	n	c	e			

1. to report to; to state or give notice
2. spoke against; gave up or rejected
3. spoke forth; declared formally or clearly
4. act of speaking out; act of speaking formally and clearly
5. act of speaking down; act of condemning a person or thing
6. messages reported to; acts of stating or giving notice
7. speaking forth incorrectly; saying a word or name wrong
8. not able to be spoken forth; not able to be declared formally
   or clearly

Spelling Bee Worries

At the bee, the <u>person who reports</u> calls out a word for the next contestant: *savanna*. "S-A-V... S-A-V-A-N-A-H." The bell dings. The judge makes an <u>outward statement</u>: Not correct. Beryl's competitor sits down. Now there are only four left. Victory is so close she can feel it. Beryl's mind begins to wander as the words are <u>spoken forth</u> one by one to the others. So close to winning, and she begins to worry. "What if in <u>stating</u> the word <u>to</u> me, the moderator doesn't <u>speak out</u> clearly? What if my mom was <u>speaking forth incorrectly</u> some of the study words? What if I don't know what he's asking?"

Another round is <u>spoken to</u> the contestants. *Coniferous, deciduous.* "Okay," thought Beryl. " I know all of those from science." *Omnipotent.* "Got that one. I just hope my word is an easy one like those." The moderator <u>speaks forth</u> Beryl's word. *Encyclopedia.* "His <u>act of speaking</u> out is clear, and I know those roots and prefixes." Beryl starts to spell, <u>speaking out</u> precisely and in a calm voice says *e-n-c-y-c-l-o-p-e-d-i-a.* "Whew, no bell, no <u>act of speaking back or rejecting</u>. I'm safe for another round!"

<u>Fill in the blanks with words from the **nounc, nounce, nunci** family.</u>

1. At the spelling bee the _____ called out the words.

2. The judge made a _____ that the first speller was not correct.

3. As the words are _____ clearly to the spellers, Beryl's mind wanders.

4. Beryl hopes that the moderator while _____ the word will _____ it clearly.

5. Another worry of Beryl was that her mother might have been _____ some the study words.

6. Words such as *coniferous* and *deciduous* were _____ in the next round.

7. The moderator _____ the next word and his _____ is clear.

8. The contestant spells calmly, _____ each letter precisely.

9. The last word was correct and no bell of _____ was heard.

<u>Word Bank</u>

announced	denounce	enunciating	mispronounces	pronounces
announcer	enunciation	mispronounce	pronounced	renounced
announcing	enunciate	mispronouncing	pronouncement	renunciation

www.dynamicliteracy.com

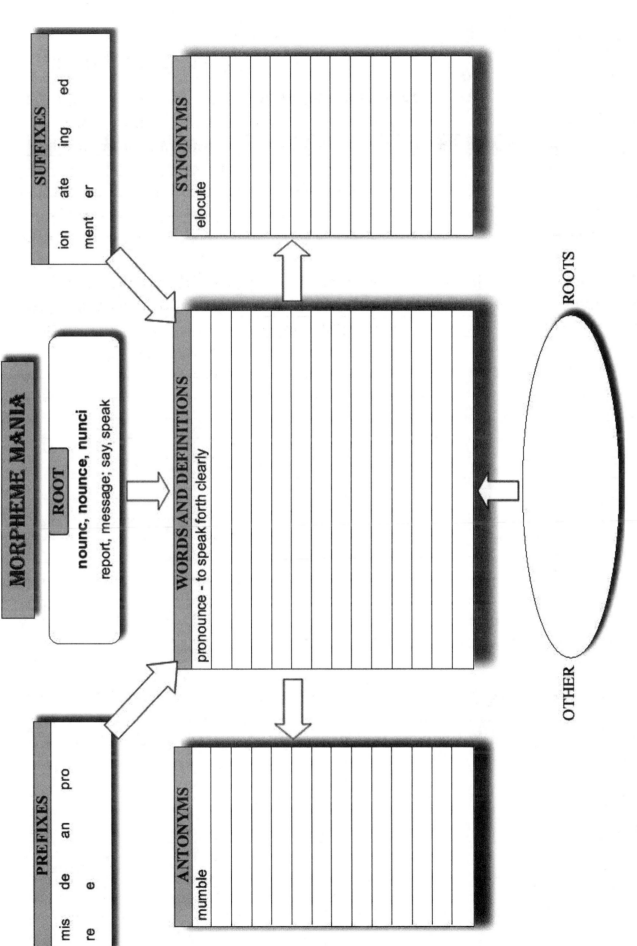

MORPHEME MANIA

PREFIXES
mis   an   pro
de   e
re

SUFFIXES
ion   ate   ing   ed
ment   er

ROOT
nounc, nounce, nunci
report, message; say, speak

WORDS AND DEFINITIONS
pronounce - to speak forth clearly

SYNONYMS
elocute

ANTONYMS
mumble

ROOTS
OTHER

Build as many words as you can for this root family. Use the prefixes and suffixes listed, or add your own. If you use any "combining roots", add them to the "Other Roots" box. Try to think of an antonym and a synonym for each word you build.

www.DynamicLiteracy.com

Root: *nounc, nounce, nunci*

Word	Synonym / Antonym	Word	Synonym / Antonym

Morphemes for this meaning family

Prefixes	Roots	Suffixes

Root Squares

How many words can you make?

Start in any square. Your goal is to combine two or more word parts to make as many words in the 'clud, clude, clus, cluse' family as you can. Write each word and a definition you can think of for it in the space provided at the bottom of the page.

ly	re	in
se	clud, clude, clus, cluse	ion
con	ive	ex

_____

_____

_____

_____

_____

_____

_____

_____

_____

Magic Squares

Select the best answer for each of the words in the 'clud, clude, clus, cluse' family from the numbered definitions. Put the number in the proper space in the Magic Square box. If the total of the numbers is the same both across and down, you have found the magic number!

'clud, clude, clus, cluse' means to shut

WORDS	DEFINITIONS
A. conclusion	1. acts or processes of shutting in; acts of containing or involving
B. conclusive	2. to shut out; to bar from participation
C. exclude	3. behaving in a way that shuts oneself back; tending to want to be alone
D. exclusively	4. tending to shut in; tending to contain or involve
E. inclusive	5. shapes, appearances, or arrangements
F. preclude	6. to shut off beforehand; to hinder or prevent
G. reclusive	7. the act or process of shutting completely; an act of ending or finishing
H. seclusion	8. in a manner tending to shut out; so as to bar from participation
I. secluded	9. tending to shut completely; tending to end or finish
	10. shut off or away; hidden or isolated

Magic Square Box

A.	B.	C.
D.	E.	F.
G.	H.	I.

Magic Number ____

Stair Steps

Fill in the missing letters of each CLUD, CLUDE, CLUS, CLUSE word
by using the definitions below.
CLUD, CLUDE, CLUS, CLUSE means to shut

1.		c	l	u	d	e					
2.		c	l	u	d						
3.		c	l	u	s						
4.			c	l	u	s					
5.			c	l	u	s					
6.			c	l	u	s					
7.			c	l	u	s					
8.					c	l	u	s			

1. to shut in; to contain or involve
2. shut off or away; hidden or isolated
3. behaving in a way that shuts oneself back; tending to want to be alone
4. the act or process of shutting completely; an act of ending or finishing
5. in a manner tending to shut out; so as to bar from participation
6. in a manner tending to shut completely; in a manner tending to end or finish
7. state of shutting out others
8. in a manner unable to be shut off or ended

 At the Country Club

Most people find it easier to relax in a <u>hidden or shut off</u> place. Many people who can afford it join a County Club, because the membership tends to <u>shut in or contain</u> people similar to them and <u>shut out</u> people who are different. Membership in a private club <u>shuts off or prevents</u> non-members from entry. The only problem with such <u>a state of shutting out others</u> is that you may miss the chance to meet someone wonderful. Even a <u>person who shut himself back by choosing to be alone most of the time</u> needs to emerge from <u>the act of shutting off</u> once in a while to explore new experiences. In <u>acting to shut off or end this story</u>, Country Clubs are described as <u>tending to shut out</u>, not <u>tending to shut in</u>.

<u>Fill in the blanks using words from the **clud**, **clude**, **clus**, **cluse** family.</u>

1. Most people like to find a _____ place where they can relax.

2. Some clubs tend to _____ members who are all similar to each other.

3. Clubs like that tend to _____ people who don't fit in in some way.

4. The membership requirement _____ non-members from entering.

5. Such _____ of a club can prevent a person from getting to know people who are different.

6. A person who is a _____ needs to try to get out and have new experiences.

7. Everyone needs to break out of _____ once in a while.

8. In _____, we are saying that people need to be around others at least some of the time.

9. Clubs that keep certain people out are described as _____.

10. Clubs that allow all different kinds of people in are described as _____.

<u>Word Bank</u>

conclude	exclusive	inconclusive	secluded
conclusion	exclusiveness	precludes	secluding
conclusively	include	recluse	seclusion
exclude	inclusive	reclusively	seclusions

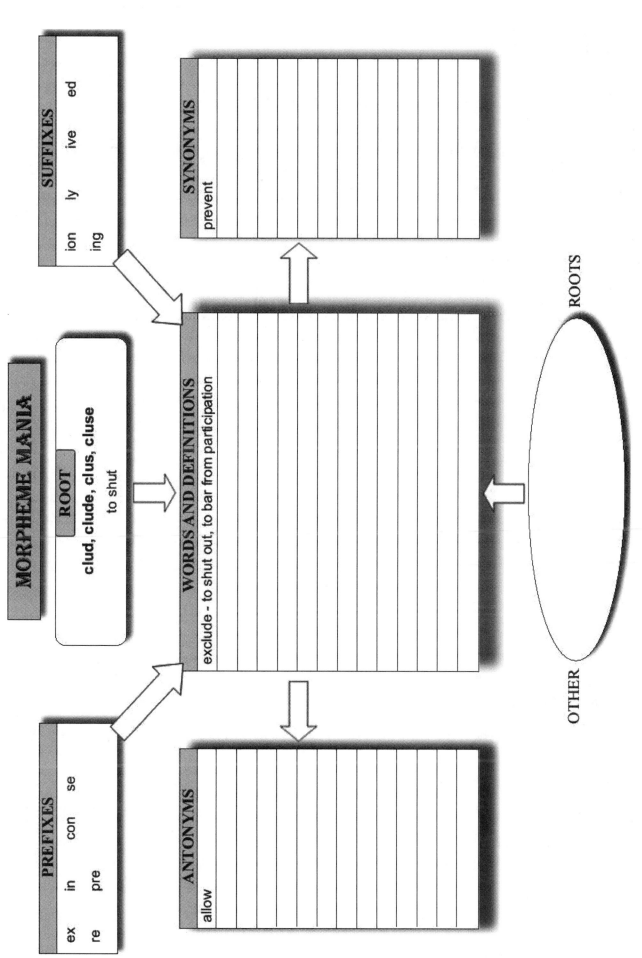

MORPHEME MANIA

PREFIXES

ex	in	con	se
re	pre		

SUFFIXES

ion	ly	ive	ed
ing			

ROOT

clud, clude, clus, cluse

to shut

WORDS AND DEFINITIONS

exclude - to shut out, to bar from participation

SYNONYMS

prevent

ANTONYMS

allow

OTHER ROOTS

Build as many words as you can for this root family. Use the prefixes and suffixes listed, or add your own. If you use any "combining roots", add them to the "Other Roots" box. Try to think of an antonym and a synonym for each word you build.

www.DynamicLiteracy.com

Root: *clud, clued, clus, cluse*

Word	Synonym / Antonym	Word	Synonym / Antonym

Morphemes for this meaning family

Prefixes	Roots	Suffixes

Root Squares

How many words can you make?

Start in any square. Your goal is to combine two or more word parts to make as many words in the 'it' family as you can. Write each word and a definition you can think of for it in the space provided at the bottom of the page.

in	ious	amb
trans	it	ive
ial	circu	iate

_____

_____

_____

_____

_____

_____

_____

_____

Magic Squares

Select the best answer for each of the words in the 'it' family from the numbered definitions. Put the number in the proper space in the Magic Square box. If the total of the numbers is the same both across and down, you have found the magic number!

'it' means to go; travel; passage

<table>
<tr><td>WORDS</td><td>DEFINITIONS</td></tr>
<tr><td>A. circuitous</td><td>1. going into; beginning</td></tr>
<tr><td>B. exited</td><td>2. going together as a match; agreeing or fitting</td></tr>
<tr><td>C. initial</td><td>3. tending to go across; lasting only briefly</td></tr>
<tr><td>D. intransitive</td><td>4. having action go across; having a direct object</td></tr>
<tr><td>E. initiated</td><td>5. related to going around; indirect</td></tr>
<tr><td>F. initializing</td><td>6. quality of going around about; strong motivation and determination to achieve</td></tr>
<tr><td>G. transitive</td><td>7. went out</td></tr>
<tr><td>H. ambition</td><td>8. went into; began; made as a member</td></tr>
<tr><td>I. circuit</td><td>9. relating to going in; first or beginning</td></tr>
<tr><td></td><td>10. state or quality of going across; adaptation or change</td></tr>
<tr><td></td><td>11. a passage around</td></tr>
<tr><td></td><td>12. not having action go across; lacking a direct object</td></tr>
</table>

Magic Square Box

A.	B.	C.
D.	E.	F.
G.	H.	I.

Magic Number ____

Stair Steps

Fill in the missing letters of each IT word
by using the definitions below.
IT means to go; travel; passage

1.		i	t							
2.		i	t							
3.		i	t							
4.				i	t					
5.			i	t						
6.				i	t					
7.		i	t							
8.				i	t					

1. goes out
2. went out
3. relating to going in; first or beginning
4. acts of going across; passages
5. eager to go about; motivated and determined to achieve
6. related to going around; indirect
7. goes into; begins
8. related to going across; related to adaptation or change

Ms. Higgins Is a Winner!

It takes a lot of <u>going around</u> to run for President, and finally Claudia Higgins decided she would <u>go into</u> her campaign in her hometown and jump on the <u>roundabout-going</u> of baby-hugging and back-slapping to collect votes. Avoiding planes and limos, she <u>went across</u> all over the country in simple vehicles, <u>put her beginning letters</u> on thousands of county fair programs, and won!

This would be the <u>beginning</u> time a woman ever won, and during the <u>coming out</u> interviews of the voters, most people said they thought it was worth a try.

During her <u>pertaining to passing across</u> period from president-elect to inauguration day, she planned to take the <u>going in or beginning</u> and start making some changes.

<u>Fill in the blanks using words from the **it** family.</u>

1. Ms. Higgins was _____ to run for President.

2. She _____ her run for President in her home town.

3. Candidates have to make the customary _____ around the country to meet people.

4. Ms. Higgins _____ all across the country by bus and train and even bicycle.

5. There were so many people asking for her autograph that she merely _____ what they gave her to write on.

6. Though females had run before, this was the _____ victory for women.

7. At the _____ interviews, people said they were willing to try something totally new.

8. In the _____ period between November and January, Ms. Higgins planned a program.

9. Rather than waste more time, she took the _____ to make needed changes.

<u>Word Bank</u>

adit	circuit	initialized	transited
ambition	exit	initiated	transitional
ambitious	initial	initiative	transitively

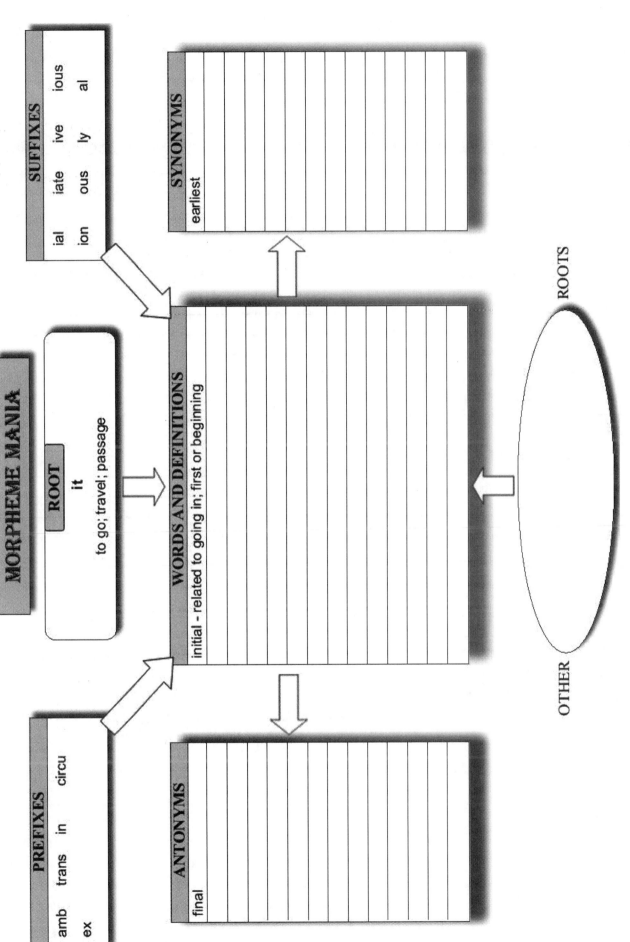

MORPHEME MANIA

PREFIXES

amb	trans	in	circu
ex			

SUFFIXES

ial	iate	ive	ious
ion	ous	ly	al

ROOT

it

to go; travel; passage

WORDS AND DEFINITIONS

initial – related to going in; first or beginning

SYNONYMS

earliest

ANTONYMS

final

ROOTS

OTHER

Build as many words as you can for this root family. Use the prefixes and suffixes listed, or add your own. If you use any "combining roots", add them to the "Other Roots" box. Try to think of an antonym and a synonym for each word you build.

www.DynamicLiteracy.com

Root: *it*

Word	Synonym / Antonym	Word	Synonym / Antonym

Morphemes for this meaning family

Prefixes	Roots	Suffixes

Root Squares

How many words can you make?

Start in any square. Your goal is to combine two or more word parts to make as many words in the 'pot, pos, poss' family as you can. Write each word and a definition you can think of for it in the space provided at the bottom of the page.

ib	sess	ence
ial	pot, pos, poss	ly
ent	ive	omni

_____

_____

_____

_____

_____

_____

_____

_____

_____

www.dynamicliteracy.com

Magic Squares

Select the best answer for each of the words in the 'pot, pos, poss' family from the numbered definitions. Put the number in the proper space in the Magic Square box. If the total of the numbers is the same both across and down, you have found the magic number!

'pot, pos, poss' means powerful, able

WORDS
A. impossibilities
B. omnipotence
C. possess
D. possibility
E. potentate
F. repossessed
G. potentials
H. posse
I. possession

DEFINITIONS
1. characterized by power or ability; aptitude
2. quality of being all-powerful
3. act of settling upon with power; something owned
4. act or quality of being in one's power to do
5. powers or abilities; aptitudes
6. powerful lord or leader
7. to settle upon with power; to own
8. sat upon again with power of ownership
9. acts or qualities not in one's power to do
10. a group given legal power for a specific task

Magic Square Box

A.	B.	C.
D.	E.	F.
G.	H.	I.

Magic Number ____

www.dynamicliteracy.com

Stair Steps

Fill in the missing letters of each POT, POS, POSS word
by using the definitions below.
POT, POS, POSS means powerful, able

1.	p	o	t								
2.	p	o	s	s							
3.			p	o	s						
4.	p	o	s								
5.	p	o	t								
6.				p	o	t					
7.			p	o	s	s					
8.	p	o	s								

1. power or ability
2. so as to be in one's power to do
3. to sit upon again with power of ownership
4. eager to settle upon with power; tending to want to own
5. in a manner characterized by power or ability
6. in an all-powerful manner
7. act or quality of not being in one's power to do
8. eagerness to settle upon with power of ownership

Manhunt

After Lousy Larry escaped from jail, the town formed a <u>group given legal power for a specific task</u> to catch him. Some said he was too clever and it would be <u>not in one's power</u> to catch him. It was said he <u>settled upon with power, or owned</u> vast and <u>powerful</u> intelligence and instincts that made him feel <u>all powerful</u>. The people in the group were not dummies either, and they thought it would be <u>in one's power</u> to <u>sit upon Larry again with power of ownership</u>. After two months, the group thought about giving up because Larry had the help of many <u>powerful lords or leaders</u> to help him cover his tracks. Then they got their big break. It was well known that Larry had a sweet tooth. He had to <u>settle upon with power, or own</u> a certain type of candy. The group had reliable information that he was in Dodge City, and there was only one store in town that carried Larry's favorite candy. The group hid outside the candy store for two days until Larry finally came in and they <u>sat upon him again with power of ownership</u>. The moral of the story? Your mom always told you that sweets were bad for you!

<u>Fill in the blanks with words from the **pot**, **pos**, **poss** family.</u>

1. The sheriff of a town sometimes forms a _____ to help catch crooks.

2. Some people thought that it was _____ to catch this particular crook.

3. Lousy Larry is said to have _____ uncanny instincts.

4. He also had an incredibly _____ intelligence and memory

5. Lousy Larry felt _____ because of his superiority.

6. The sheriff and his helpers faithfully believed that it was _____ to catch Lousy Larry, and that they would do it.

7. They planned to _____ Lousy Larry and bring him back to jail.

8. The criminal had help from a lot of strong and wealthy _____.

9. Every crook has a weak spot. Lousy Larry's was that he had to _____ at all times a certain type of candy.

10. With the bait of candy, the law _____ Larry and took him back to jail.

Word Bank

impossibilities	omnipotent	possessed	potent
impossible	posse	possible	potentates
impotence	possess	potency	repossess
potentially	potentials	repossessed	potentials

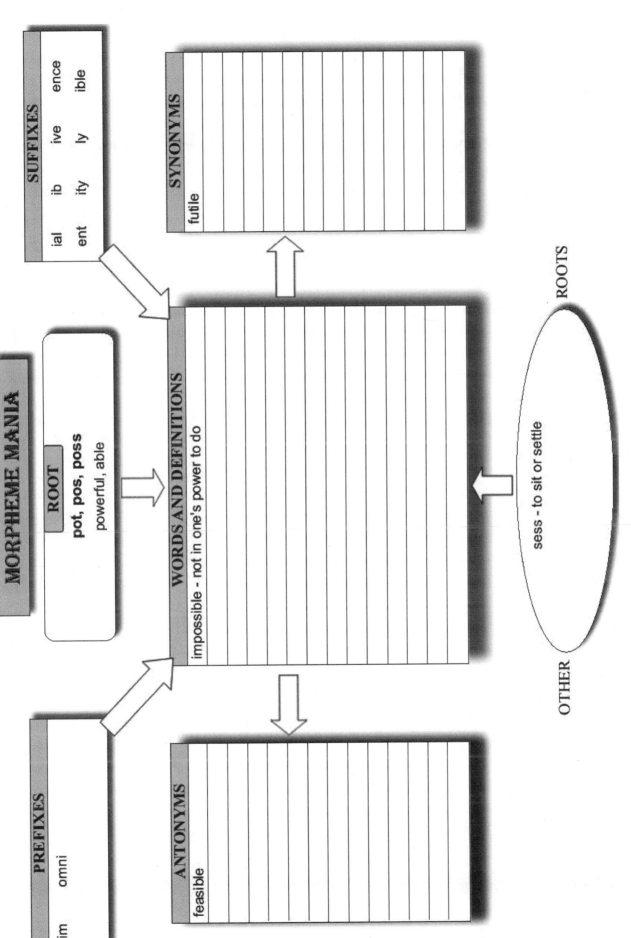

MORPHEME MANIA

PREFIXES

im

omni

SUFFIXES

ial	ib	ive	ence
ent	ity	ly	ible

ROOT

pot, pos, poss

powerful, able

WORDS AND DEFINITIONS

impossible - not in one's power to do

SYNONYMS

futile

ANTONYMS

feasible

OTHER ROOTS

sess - to sit or settle

Build as many words as you can for this root family. Use the prefixes and suffixes listed, or add your own. If you use any "combining roots", add them to the "Other Roots" box. Try to think of an antonym and a synonym for each word you build.

www.DynamicLiteracy.com

Root: *pot, pos, poss*

Word	Synonym / Antonym	Word	Synonym / Antonym

Morphemes for this meaning family

Prefixes	Roots	Suffixes

Root Squares

How many words can you make?

Start in any square. Your goal is to combine two or more word parts to make as many words in the 'merg, merge, mers, merse' family as you can. Write each word and a definition you can think of for it in the space provided at the bottom of the page.

sub	im	es
y	merg, merge, mers, merse	ible
e	ence	er

_____

_____

_____

_____

_____

_____

_____

_____

Magic Squares

Select the best answer for each of the words in the 'merg, merge, mers, merse' family from the numbered definitions. Put the number in the proper space in the Magic Square box. If the total of the numbers is the same both across and down, you have found the magic number!

'merg, merge, mers, merse' means to sink into or beneath the surface

WORDS	DEFINITIONS
A. emergencies	1. arose from beneath the surface; surface
B. emerging	2. sank into
C. immerging	3. an arising from beneath the surface; surfacing
D. immersible	4. pertaining to an item that will sink below
E. submersing	5. sank or was absorbed into something else; became as one or alike
F. submersal	6. sank below
G. merging	7. serious events that arise suddenly; sudden and critical events
H. emergence	8. sinking into
I. merge	9. sinking or being absorbed into something else; becoming as one or alike
	10. capable of being sunk into water with no damage
	11. coming into being from beneath the surface; surfacing
	12. causing to sink below
	13. acts of sinking or absorbing into something else; unions
	14. to sink or be absorbed into something else; to become as one or alike

Magic Square Box

A.	B.	C.
D.	E.	F.
G.	H.	I.

Magic Number ____

www.dynamicliteracy.com

Stair Steps

Fill in the missing letters of each MERG, MERGE, MERS, MERSE word by using the definitions below.

MERG, MERGE, MERS, MERSE means to sink into or beneath the surface

1. | m | e | r | g |
2. | m | e | r | g |
3. | | | m | e | r | s |
4. | | | | m | e | r | g | e |
5. | | | m | e | r | s |
6. | | | | m | e | r | g |
7. | | | m | e | r | s |
8. | m | e | r | g |
9. | | | | m | e | r | g |

1. the sinking or absorbing into something else; a union
2. sinking or being absorbed into something else; becoming as one or alike
3. sank beneath the surface of a liquid
4. to sink below
5. sinking beneath the surface of a liquid
6. sank below
7. capable of being sunk into water with no damage
8. serious events that arise suddenly; sudden and critical events
9. acts or processes of sinking below

At the Scene of the Accident

The serious event that arises quickly happened so fast. A car attempted to be absorbed with traffic but was cut off by another car. The first car bounced off a truck, flew off the bridge, and sank beneath the surface of the river. The straps holding the load on the truck broke, and the cargo, a vehicle able to operate beneath the surface, also slid into the river. This was a stroke of good luck because the first car was not capable of being sunk into water with no damage and sank quickly. It was a good thing I had experience as a diver. I dived into the water, and as soon as I sank below I could see the car sinking into the water and the other vehicle surfacing from below. I quickly climbed on the vehicle and raced toward the sinking car. I got the driver and her dog out, and as we arose from beneath the surface, a cheer went up from the crowd that had gathered to watch.

Fill in the blanks with words from the **merg, merge, mers, merse** family.

1. An _____ can happen so suddenly.

2. It is not an easy matter to _____ into fast-moving traffic.

3. A car was hit with such force that it was _____ in the river.

4. Luckily, a _____ vehicle was also pushed beneath the river.

5. Cars are normally not _____ in water.

6. As soon as I was _____ under the water, I saw both vehicles.

7. One car was _____ downward into the water, and the other was _____ up from below.

8. We all were cheered when we safely _____ from the water.

Word Bank

emerge	emerging	immersible	submerged
emerged	immerging	merge	submergence
emergency	immersed	mergers	submersible

MORPHEME MANIA

PREFIXES

| im | sub | e |

SUFFIXES

| er | es | y | ible |
| enc | ed | ion | |

ROOT

merg, merge, mers, merse

to sink into or beneath the surface

WORDS AND DEFINITIONS

emerge - to arise from beneath the surface

SYNONYMS

gush

ANTONYMS

sink

ROOTS

OTHER

Build as many words as you can for this root family. Use the prefixes and suffixes listed, or add your own. If you use any "combining roots", add them to the "Other Roots" box. Try to think of an antonym and a synonym for each word you build.

www.DynamicLiteracy.com

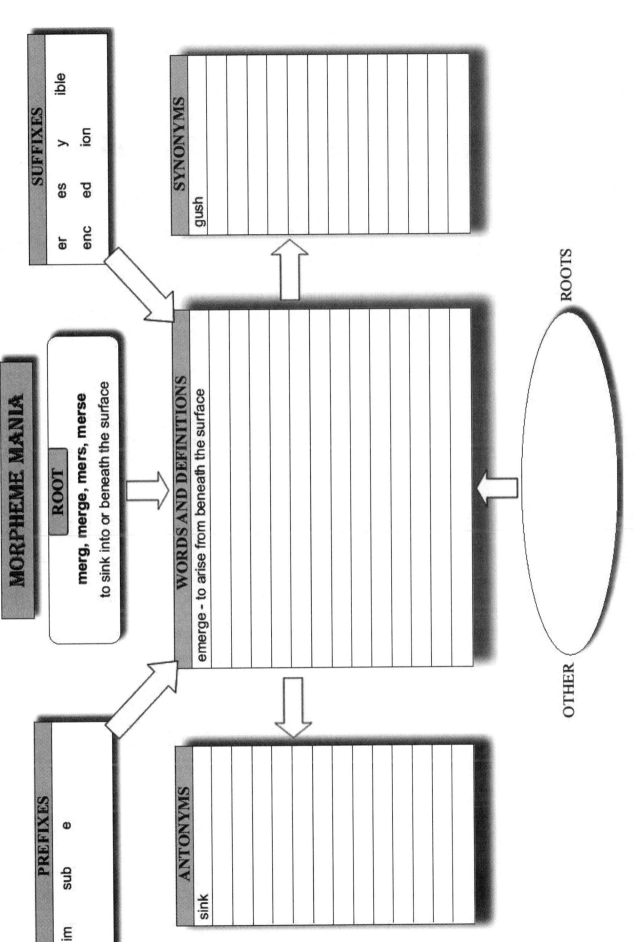

Root: *merg, merge, mers, merse*

Word	Synonym / Antonym	Word	Synonym / Antonym

Morphemes for this meaning family

Prefixes	Roots	Suffixes

Stair Steps

Fill in the missing letters of each MAND, MEND
word by using the definitions below.
MAND, MEND means to order; to put into someone's hand; entrust to

1.		m	a	n	d					
2.			m	a	n	d				
3.	m	a	n	d						
4.	m	a	n	d						
5.		m	a	n	d					
6.		m	e	n	d					
7.		m	a	n	d					
8.					m	a	n	d		
9.				m	e	n	d			

1. to order from; to request forcefully or insist
2. to give orders to; an order that is given
3. official orders
4. required by official order; necessary
5. people who give orders
6. able to be trusted; praiseworthy
7. powerful orders
8. reversed an order
9. an act of praising again as trustworthy

Trust Me!

This is a story from my days as a member of a <u>fighting unit that has been given special orders</u>. The <u>person who gives orders</u> on my team <u>forcefully ordered</u> that we all attend a <u>necessary</u> meeting. Even though he asked us to <u>praise as trustworthy</u> plans for a rescue mission, we knew that he was in charge and would make the final decision on our plan. An hour later, we boarded a plane at a secret location and headed off on the mission. Once we landed, my job was to free two hostages, then head south to meet the rest of the team. I found the hostages and <u>gave orders to</u> them to follow me, but we soon discovered the road to the south was blocked. In that moment, I had to decide whether I should <u>reverse</u> his <u>order</u>, or follow his order. I chose to go the opposite direction he had told me to go, and I was able to get the hostages to safety. Later, when we discussed what had happened, he <u>praised</u> me for thinking well under pressure and adjusting his <u>official order</u> to fit the situation I had encountered.

<u>Fill in the blanks using words from the **mand, mend** family.</u>

1. I once served as a team member of a _____ unit.

2. Each team was led by a _____ .

3. That leader _____ that we attend a meeting to hear the orders.

4. The meeting was _____, and there would be no excuse for missing it.

5. The leader allowed us to _____ various plans for a rescue mission.

6. After I located the hostages, I _____ them to follow me.

7. I suddenly had to decide whether to obey or to _____ my leader.

8. It is a serious matter not to follow a direct _____.

9. Rather than be angry with me, the leader _____ me for my quick thinking.

10. I had changed the original _____ and by doing so saved lives.

Word Bank

command	commanding	commended	mandatory
commandants	commando	countermand	recommend
commanded	commendable	demanded	recommendation
commander	commendation	mandate	recommends

www.dynamicliteracy.com

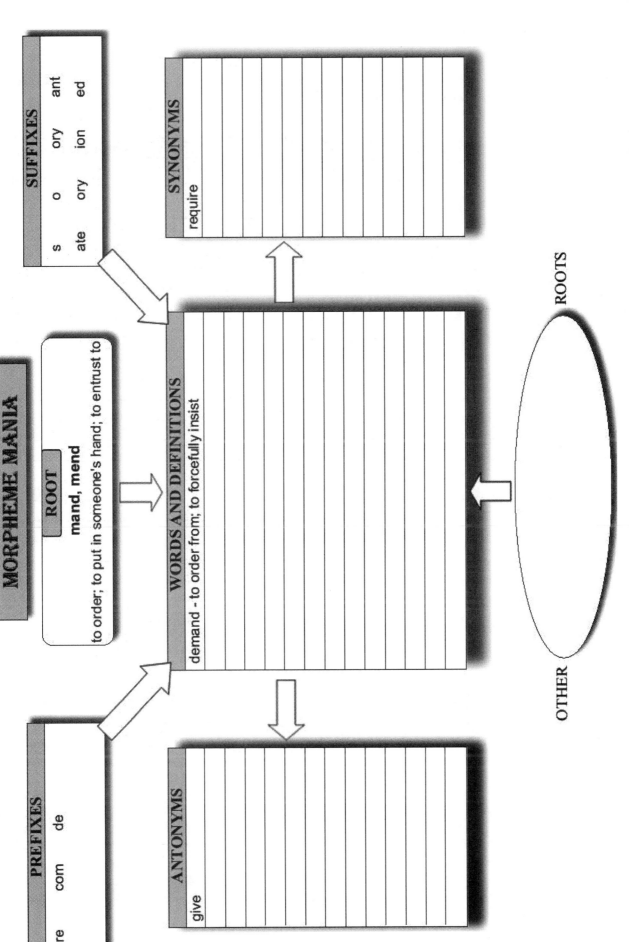

MORPHEME MANIA

PREFIXES

re   com   de

SUFFIXES

s   o   ory   ant

ate   ory   ion   ed

ROOT

mand, mend

to order; to put in someone's hand; to entrust to

WORDS AND DEFINITIONS

demand – to order from; to forcefully insist

SYNONYMS

require

ANTONYMS

give

OTHER ROOTS

Build as many words as you can for this root family. Use the prefixes and suffixes listed, or add your own. If you use any "combining roots", add them to the "Other Roots" box. Try to think of an antonym and a synonym for each word you build.

www.DynamicLiteracy.com

Root: *mand, mend*

Word	Synonym / Antonym	Word	Synonym / Antonym

Morphemes for this meaning family

Prefixes	Roots	Suffixes

Root Squares

How many words can you make?

Start in any square. Your goal is to combine two or more word parts to make as many words in the 'rupt' family as you can. Write each word and a definition you can think of for it in the space provided at the bottom of the page.

inter	ure	dis
ion	rupt	cor
ab	e	ive

_____

_____

_____

_____

_____

_____

_____

_____

Magic Squares

Select the best answer for each of the words in the 'rupt' family from the numbered definitions. Put the number in the proper space in the Magic Square box. If the total of the numbers is the same both across and down, you have found the magic number!

'rupt' means to break

WORDS	DEFINITIONS
A. abruptly	1. act or process of causing to break apart; act of throwing into confusion
B. disruptive	2. breaks out; explodes
C. erupts	3. broke into; cut in and brought to a stop
D. eruption	4. act or process of breaking out; explosion
E. interruptions	5. to break; to explode or split open
F. corruption	6. the state of being thoroughly broken; process of becoming dishonest and unprincipled
G. rupture	7. tending to cause to break apart; tending to throw into confusion
H. interrupted	8. acts of breaking into; acts of cutting in or bringing to a stop
I. corrupts	9. in a manner as to break off; in an unexpectedly sudden manner
	10. thoroughly breaks; causes to become dishonest and unprincipled

Magic Square Box

A.	B.	C.
D.	E.	F.
G.	H.	I.

Magic Number ____

www.dynamicliteracy.com

Stair Steps

Fill in the missing letters of each RUPT
word by using the definitions below.
RUPT means to break

	1.		r	u	p	t					
2.			r	u	p	t					
3.				r	u	p	t				
4.			r	u	p	t					
5.	r	u	p	t							
6.			r	u	p	t					
7.			r	u	p	t					
8.			r	u	p	t					
9.				r	u	p	t				

1. to break out; to explode
2. breaking off; unexpectedly sudden
3. thoroughly broken; dishonest and unprincipled
4. in a manner as to break off; in an unexpectedly sudden manner
5. acts or processes of breaking out; explosions
6. act or process of causing to break apart; act of throwing into confusion
7. capable of being thoroughly broken; able to be made dishonest
8. in a manner causing to break apart; in a manner tending to throw into confusion
9. acts of breaking into; acts of cutting in and bringing to a stop

The <u>act of breaking out</u> of Mt. Vesuvius in the year 79 caused a deadly <u>act of breaking apart</u> in the lives of many people in the city of Pompeii. Although people's daily routines had not been <u>broken into</u> by some earth tremors in the area several days before, people did not <u>break apart</u> their overall way of life. The volcano <u>broke out</u> so <u>in a manner as if broken off</u> that most people had no chance to escape. It was as if the earth was <u>splitting open</u>. An <u>unexpectedly sudden</u> wall of thick ash buried the entire city as the citizens were going about their business.

As often happens in a disaster, there were those afterward who shouted that Pompeii was punished for its <u>state of being thoroughly broken and dishonest</u>. Nature, however, does not know or care that it is sometimes a great <u>instrument that causes a breaking apart</u> to humankind.

<u>Fill in the blanks using words from the **rupt** family.</u>

1. There was an _____ of Mt. Vesuvius in the year 79.

2. Disasters can cause a deadly _____ of the lives of their victims.

3. They thought the tremors merely _____ their day temporarily.

4. The tremors did not at all _____ their overall way of life.

5. Mt. Vesuvius _____ with tremendous force.

6. Death came _____ for most people.

7. The earth seemed simply to be _____.

8. The wall of thick ash was _____ and unexpected.

9. Some people took the luxury of Pompeii to be a sign of wickedness and _____.

10. Nature is not aware that it is a _____ to the inhabitants of earth.

Word Bank

abrupt	corruption	erupted	interrupted
abruptly	disrupt	eruption	interruptions
corrupt	disruption	disruptor	rupturing

www.dynamicliteracy.com

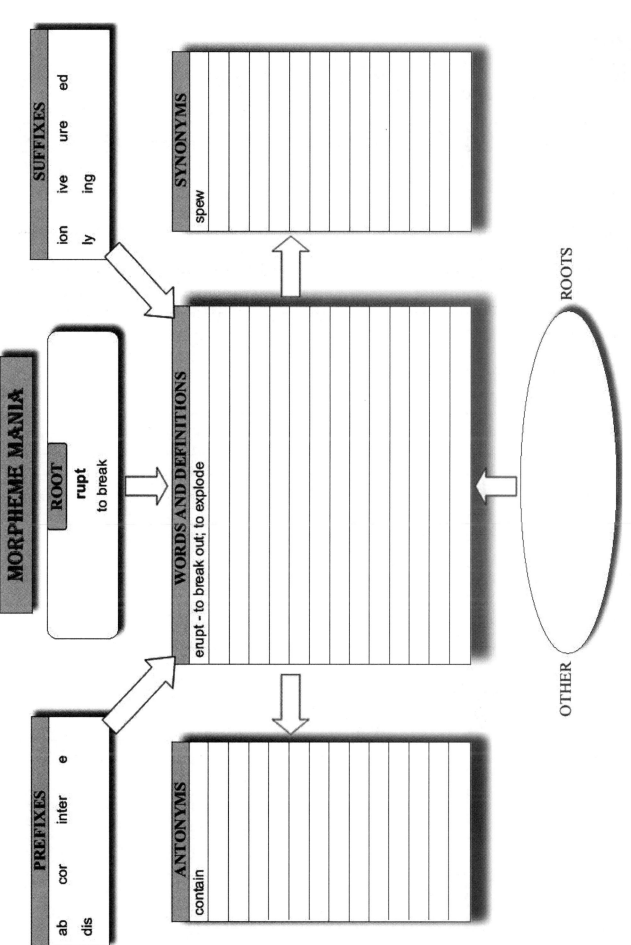

MORPHEME MANIA

PREFIXES

ab   inter   e

dis

SUFFIXES

ion   ive   ure   ed

ly   ing

ROOT

rupt
to break

WORDS AND DEFINITIONS

erupt – to break out; to explode

SYNONYMS

spew

ANTONYMS

contain

OTHER ROOTS

Build as many words as you can for this root family. Use the prefixes and suffixes listed, or add your own. If you use any "combining roots", add them to the "Other Roots" box. Try to think of an antonym and a synonym for each word you build.

www.DynamicLiteracy.com

My Word Wall

Name

Root: *rupt*

Word	Synonym / Antonym	Word	Synonym / Antonym

Morphemes for this meaning family

Prefixes	Roots	Suffixes

Root Squares

How many words can you make?

Start in any square. Your goal is to combine two or more word parts to make as many words in the 'cur, curr, curs' family as you can. Write each word and a definition you can think of for it in the space provided at the bottom of the page.

ence	oc	or
pre	cur, curr, curs	ion
con	ex	y

_____

_____

_____

_____

_____

_____

_____

_____

Magic Squares

Select the best answer for each of the words in the 'cur, curr, curs' family from the numbered definitions. Put the number in the proper space in the Magic Square box. If the total of the numbers is the same both across and down, you have found the magic number!

'cur, curr, curs' means to run

WORDS
A. concurrently
B. currently
C. cursively
D. cursory
E. precursors
F. excursions
G. recurrent
H. occurs
I. incur

DEFINITIONS
1. running; hasty, without close attention
2. type of money "running"; the form of money used in a country
3. a running up against; a happening
4. to run into; to acquire or attain
5. so as to run; in a flowing manner, as with handwriting
6. runs up against; happens
7. in a running manner; happening now
8. things running before; forerunners or omens
9. in a manner running together; so as to occur at the same time
10. runs back; takes place again
11. running back; happening again
12. acts of running out; vacations or adventures

Magic Square Box

A.	B.	C.
D.	E.	F.
G.	H.	I.

Magic Number ____

www.dynamicliteracy.com

Stair Steps

Fill in the missing letters of each CUR, CURR, CURS
word by using the definitions below.
CUR, CURR, CURS means to run

1. | | | c | u | r | | | | |
2. | | | c | u | r | | | | |
3. | c | u | r | s | | | | | |
4. | c | u | r | r | | | | | |
5. | | c | u | r | r | | | | |
6. | | | c | u | r | s | | | |
7. | | c | u | r | s | | | | |
8. | | c | u | r | r | | | | |
9. | | | c | u | r | r | | | |

1. to run back; to happen again
2. runs into; acquires or attains
3. running; flowing smoothly, as with handwriting
4. type of money "running"; the form of money used in a country
5. ran up against; happened
6. whatever runs before; a forerunner or omen
7. acts of running out; vacations or adventures
8. events that run back; acts of happening again
9. in a manner running together; so as to occur at the same time

A Dream Come True

Tobias had a <u>running back over again</u> dream. Every night he dreamt that he received a letter in beautiful <u>smoothly flowing</u> handwriting. He would only <u>as if running</u> read the note but thought that it invited him to go on a <u>vacation, running out</u> down a river. He would go to the river but the <u>flowing</u> was too dangerous and he would turn back. Tobias' doctor, after hearing a description of the dream, gave a long explanation <u>running in different directions</u> that the dream was a <u>forerunner</u> to his <u>running into</u> debt. Then the doctor gave him a beautifully written bill requiring that Tobias gather up a huge amount of <u>circulating money</u>. That's when it <u>ran up against</u> Tobias that he had been cleverly tricked, but he had to <u>run along with or agree</u> with his doctor that the dream had come true.

<u>Fill in the blanks using words from the **cur**, **curr**, **curs** family.</u>

1. Tobias' dream was a _____ one, happening every night.

2. The note which Tobias was given in every dream was in a beautiful _____ script.

3. He would only _____ read the note but understood that he was to take a trip.

4. The trip was to be an _____ down a river.

5. Tobias felt that the _____ of the river was too dangerous.

6. The doctor gave a lengthy _____ explanation requiring a lot of time.

7. Tobias learned that the dream was indeed a _____ to being sent down the river.

8. The doctor told Tobias that he would be _____ a big debt.

9. Tobias had to gather up a great deal of _____ to pay the doctor.

10. Finally, the joke and the clever trickery _____ to Tobias.

11. Tobias had to _____ with the doctor about what the dream had meant.

<u>Word Bank</u>

concur	currency	cursive	excursion	precursor
concurrence	current	cursorily	incurring	recurring
concurrent	currently	discursive	occurred	recurs

www.dynamicliteracy.com

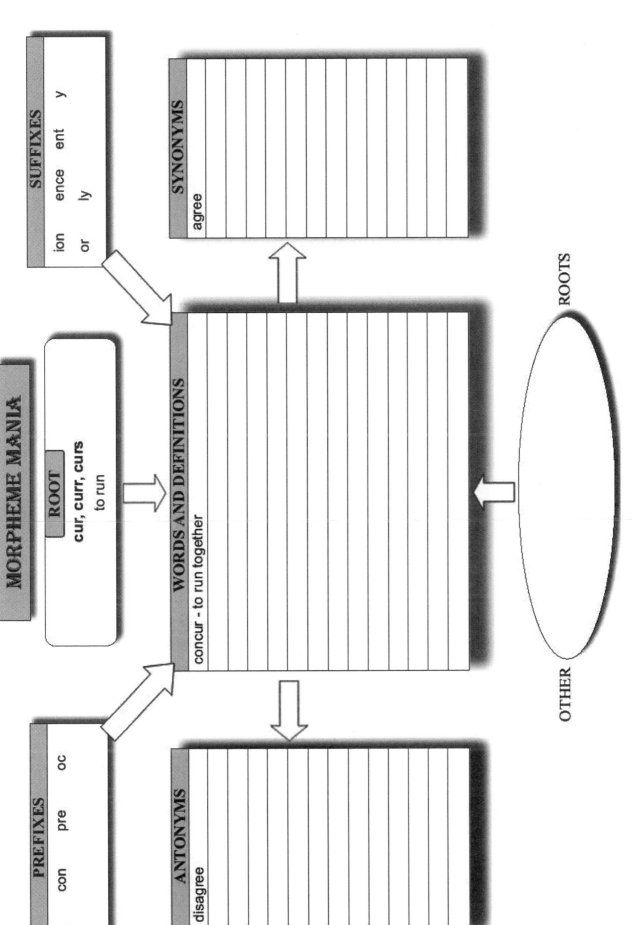

MORPHEME MANIA

PREFIXES

ex	con	oc
re	pre	

SUFFIXES

ion	ence	ent	y
or		ly	

ROOT

cur, curr, curs
to run

WORDS AND DEFINITIONS

concur – to run together

SYNONYMS

agree

ANTONYMS

disagree

OTHER ROOTS

Build as many words as you can for this root family. Use the prefixes and suffixes listed, or add your own. If you use any "combining roots", add them to the "Other Roots" box. Try to think of an antonym and a synonym for each word you build.

www.DynamicLiteracy.com

Root: *cur, curr, curs*

Word	Synonym / Antonym	Word	Synonym / Antonym

Morphemes for this meaning family

Prefixes	Roots	Suffixes

Root Squares

How many words can you make?

Start in any square. Your goal is to combine two or more word parts to make as many words in the 'fess, fant, fanti' family as you can. Write each word and a definition you can think of for it in the space provided at the bottom of the page.

semi	al	ile
pro	fess, fant, fanti	ion
un	in	ly

_____ _____ _____

_____ _____ _____

_____ _____ _____

_____ _____ _____

_____ _____ _____

_____ _____ _____

_____ _____ _____

www.dynamicliteracy.com

Magic Squares

Select the best answer for each of the words in the 'fess, fant, fanti' family from the numbered definitions. Put the number in the proper space in the Magic Square box. If the total of the numbers is the same both across and down, you have found the magic number!

'fess, fant, fanti' means to speak

<u>WORDS</u>

A. confession
B. infantile
C. nonprofessional
D. paraprofessional
E. profess
F. profession
G. unprofessionally
H. infantry
I. professional

<u>DEFINITIONS</u>

1. a person who speaks for a cause or topic; a teacher in higher education
2. act of speaking with someone; act of admitting or owning up to
3. an authority who speaks for a cause or topic; a master or expert at his or her work
4. to speak on behalf of a cause or topic; to claim
5. a group of those who do not speak; a squad of young soldiers
6. a person who works beside another who is an authority
7. a person who is not an authority to speak for a topic
8. a speaking for a cause or topic; an occupation
9. behaving as one not yet speaking; acting like a baby
10. in a manner said or done without authority; in a manner not behaving as a master or expert

Magic Square Box

A.	B.	C.
D.	E.	F.
G.	H.	I.

Magic Number _____

www.dynamicliteracy.com

Stair Steps

Fill in the missing letters of each FESS, FANT, FANTI
word by using the definitions below.

FESS, FANT, FANTI means to speak

1.			f	a	n	t						
2.				f	e	s	s					
3.		f	a	n	t							
4.			f	e	s	s						
5.			f	e	s	s						
6.		f	a	n	t							
7.			f	e	s	s						
8.			f	e	s	s						
9.					f	e	s	s				

1. one not yet speaking; a baby
2. to speak on behalf of a cause or topic; to claim
3. a group of those who do not speak; a squad of young soldiers
4. a person who speaks for a cause of topic; a teacher in higher education
5. speaking on behalf of a cause or topic; claiming
6. a condition like one not yet speaking; state of extreme immaturity
7. related to speaking with someone; pertaining to admitting or owning up to
8. authorities who speak for a cause of topic; masters or experts at their work
9. not qualified as an authority to speak on a topic; not behaving as a master or expert

Fess up!

It is perfectly normal for <u>one who is not yet speaking</u> to <u>behave as one not yet speaking</u>. However, for <u>a person who speaks for a cause or topic</u> it would be <u>not behaving as an authority to speak on a topic</u> to act in such a manner. Even <u>a person who speaks with limited authority</u> would not act <u>in a manner said or done without authority</u>.

Certainly, <u>a group of those who do not speak</u> (a squad of young soldiers) would <u>admit or own up to</u> bad behavior on their part. On the other hand, <u>a person who is not an authority to speak for a cause or topic</u> might say the wrong thing and not worry about it. Sometimes <u>speaking with someone and admitting or owning up</u> when you've done or said something wrong is very difficult.

Honesty is the best policy!

<u>Fill in the blanks using words from the **fant**, **fess** family.</u>

1. A baby is called an _____ because of its inability to speak.

2. If you act like a baby, or one not yet speaking, you are being _____.

3. College _____ speak for the topics on which they are expert.

4. It would be considered _____ for a college teacher to act like a baby.

5. A _____ speaks with limited authority on a topic.

6. Behaving _____ could cause people to be fired from their jobs!

7. Are young soldiers called _____ because they are expected to follow orders, not speak?

8. If you have done something wrong, you should _____ to someone you respect.

9. You can't always trust the advice of a person who is a _____.

10. _____, or admitting to your mistakes, takes courage.

<u>Word Bank</u>

confess	confessing	confessor	infant
infantile	infantry	nonprofessional	professors
profession	semiprofessional	unprofessional	unprofessionally

www.dynamicliteracy.com

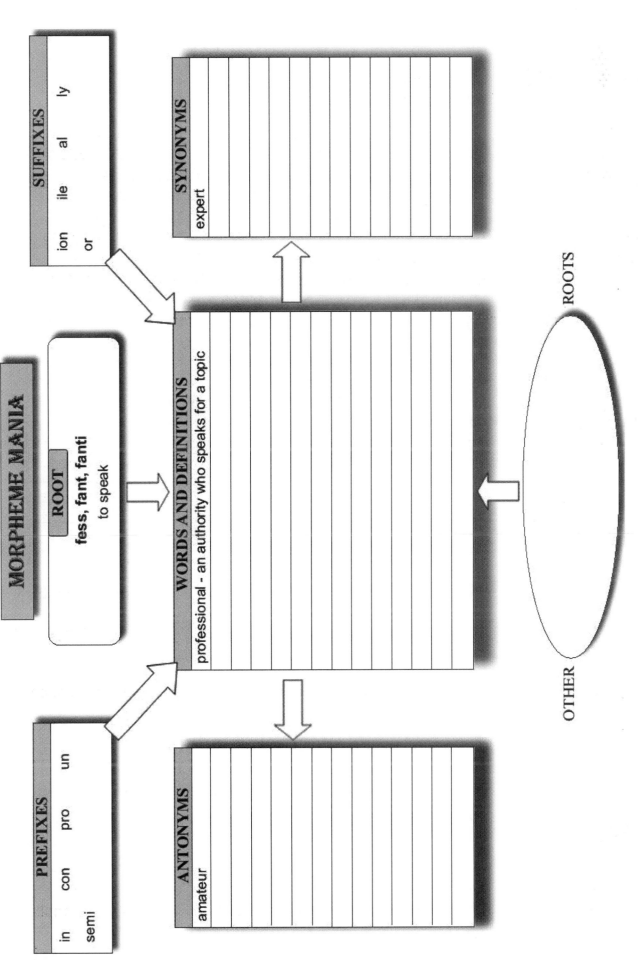

MORPHEME MANIA

SUFFIXES
ion ile al
or ly

PREFIXES
in con pro un
semi

ROOT
fess, fant, fanti
to speak

SYNONYMS
expert

WORDS AND DEFINITIONS
professional - an authority who speaks for a topic

ANTONYMS
amateur

OTHER ROOTS

Build as many words as you can for this root family. Use the prefixes and suffixes listed, or add your own. If you use any "combining roots", add them to the "Other Roots" box. Try to think of an antonym and a synonym for each word you build.

©2007 Dynamic Literacy, LLC

103

www.DynamicLiteracy.com

Root: *fess, fant, fanti*

Word	Synonym / Antonym	Word	Synonym / Antonym

Morphemes for this meaning family

Prefixes	Roots	Suffixes

Root Squares

How many words can you make?

Start in any square. Your goal is to combine two or more word parts to make as many words in the 'phon, phone, phono' family as you can. Write each word and a definition you can think of for it in the space provided at the bottom of the page.

micro	mega	caco
sym	phon, phone, phono	homo
tele	xylo	ic

_____

_____

_____

_____

_____

_____

_____

_____

Magic Squares

Select the best answer for each of the words in the 'phon, phone, phono' family from the numbered definitions. Put the number in the proper space in the Magic Square box. If the total of the numbers is the same both across and down, you have found the magic number!

'phon, phone, phono' means sound

WORDS	DEFINITIONS
A. cacophony	1. the science of sounds; application of letters sounds in reading instruction
B. homophones	2. related to 3-dimensional sound effects
C. microphone	3. people using a device to transmit sound from afar
D. phonically	4. sounding together; orchestral or in concert
E. stereophonic	5. wooden instruments that make sounds
F. symphony	6. bad, non-melodious sound
G. xylophones	7. a device for recording and reproducing sound; a record player
H. telephoning	8. small electronic device to enlarge sound
I. phonograph	9. group playing sounds together; an orchestra
	10. things sounding the same; words sounding identical to others
	11. devices for enlarging sound
	12. using a device that transmits sound from afar
	13. in a manner pertaining to the production of sound

Magic Square Box

A.	B.	C.
D.	E.	F.
G.	H.	I.

Magic Number ____

www.dynamicliteracy.com

Stair Steps

Fill in the missing letters of each PHON, PHONE, PHONO word
by using the definitions below.
PHON, PHONE, PHONO means sound

1. | p | h | o | n | e | | |
2. | p | h | o | n | | | |
3. | | | p | h | o | n | |
4. | | | | p | h | o | n |
5. | | | | p | h | o | n | e |
6. | | | | p | h | o | n | e |
7. | | | | | p | h | o | n | e |
8. | | | | | | p | h | o | n |

1. units of sound
2. the science of sounds; application of letter sounds in reading instruction
3. group playing sounds together; an orchestra
4. bad, non-melodious sound
5. a device that transmits sound from afar
6. wooden instruments that make sounds
7. small electronic devices to enlarge sound
8. related to 3-dimensional sound effects

Teresa hung up her <u>device that transmits sound from afar</u>. She was all excited because she had just been invited to hear a <u>group that plays sounds together</u> give a performance at the concert hall. She loved hearing live music because the <u>three-dimensional</u> sound was like being enveloped in music. She was also excited to go because her friend Mohsen plays the <u>wooden instrument that makes sound</u> in the <u>sounding-together</u> orchestra. He has <u>small electronic devices to enhance sound</u> next to him so that his playing can be heard along with the loud tubas and trumpets.

As Teresa sat waiting for the performance, she even enjoyed the <u>bad, non-melodious sound</u> of all the performers doing their last-minute tuning up and instrument-checking. Finally the conductor called the musicians to order through a <u>device for enlarging sound</u>, and the hall quickly quieted down for the performance.

<u>Fill in the blanks using words from the **phon, phone, phono** family.</u>

1. Teresa hung up after she had been talking with someone on her _____.

2. She had been invited to the concert hall to hear a _____.

3. Teresa loved the _____ sensation of being surrounded by music.

4. Her friend played the _____ for the orchestra.

5. His musical instrument was not as loud as the others in the _____ orchestra.

6. So that Mohsen's music could be heard, _____ were used to carry the sound of his performance.

7. All the tuning up created a dazzling _____ of sound before the performance.

8. The conductor used a _____ to talk to the musicians over their noise.

<u>Word Bank</u>

cacophony	microphones	phonograph	symphony
homophone	phonemes	stereophonic	telephone
megaphone	phonetic	symphonic	xylophone

www.dynamicliteracy.com

MORPHEME MANIA

PREFIXES

homo caco micro un

tele sym

ROOT

phon, phone, phono
sound

SUFFIXES

ic y er ed

WORDS AND DEFINITIONS

telephone - to use a device that transmits sound

SYNONYMS***

call

ANTONYMS***

ignore

*** This is a tough one for antonyms and synonyms - you will build many nouns, and they don't have antonyms or synonyms. If you can define them as verbs you can come up with antonyms and synonyms - and you're pretty smart!

OTHER ROOTS

xylo - wood

graph - something written, drawn, or recorded

Build as many words as you can for this root family. Use the prefixes and suffixes listed, or add your own. If you use any "combining roots", add them to the "Other Roots" box. Try to think of an antonym and a synonym for each word you build.

www.DynamicLiteracy.com

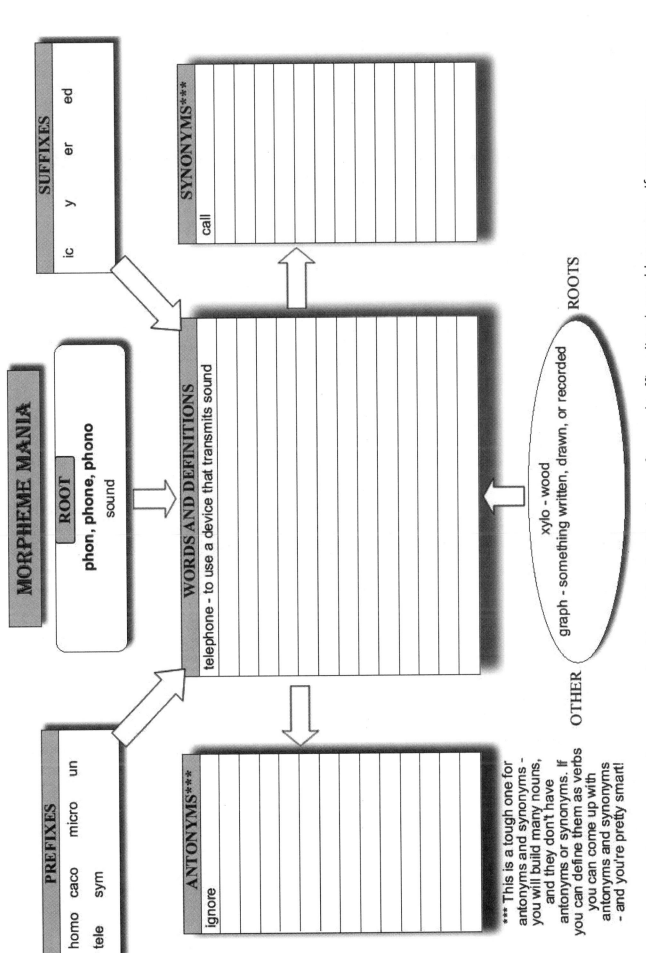

Root: *phon, phone, phono*

Word	Synonym / Antonym	Word	Synonym / Antonym

Morphemes for this meaning family

Prefixes	Roots	Suffixes

Root Squares

How many words can you make?

Start in any square. Your goal is to combine two or more word parts to make as many words in the 'art, arti, ert' family as you can. Write each word and a definition you can think of for it in the space provided at the bottom of the page.

ic	fic	ial
ity	art, arti, ert	in
ist	ness	ry

_____

_____

_____

_____

_____

_____

_____

www.dynamicliteracy.com

Magic Squares

Select the best answer for each of the words in the 'art, arti, ert' family from the numbered definitions. Put the number in the proper space in the Magic Square box. If the total of the numbers is the same both across and down, you have found the magic number!

'art, arti, ert' means skill, craft; joint; connected

WORDS
A. art
B. artfully
C. artifacts
D. artifice
E. artisans
F. inarticulate
G. inertness
H. unartistic
I. articulation

DEFINITIONS
1. something craftily made or done
2. a little piece connected; a section of a piece of writing
3. the condition of not connecting; idleness or quality of being unskillful
4. demonstrating no skill; not talented
5. in a manner of piecing together skillfully; in a talented manner
6. the act or process of piecing together skillfully; the act of putting forth words or ideas clearly
7. skillfully made objects; man-made objects of historical relevance
8. not capable of piecing together skillfully; incapable of putting forth words or ideas clearly
9. something created by putting pieces together skillfully; a product of talent
10. seeming skillfully made; contrived so as to imitate nature
11. the quality of not connecting; the quality of being idle or unskilled
12. people with skills at making things

Magic Square Box

A.	B.	C.
D.	E.	F.
G.	H.	I.

Magic Number ____

Stair Steps

Fill in the missing letters of each ART, ARTI, ERT
word by using the definitions below.
ART, ARTI, ERT means skill, craft; joint; connected

1.	a	r	t								
2.			e	r	t						
3.	a	r	t	i							
4.	a	r	t	i							
5.	a	r	t								
6.	a	r	t								
7.	a	r	t								
8.	a	r	t	i							
9.	a	r	t	i							

1. exhibiting skill at piecing together; talented
2. the condition of not connecting; idleness or quality of being unskillful
3. little pieces connected; sections of pieces of writing
4. skillfully made objects; man-made objects of historical relevance
5. skills that are demonstrated; qualities of talent
6. pieced together skillfully; jointed; put forth words or ideas clearly
7. in a manner demonstrating skill; in a talented manner
8. quality of seeming to be craftily made; quality of being contrived to imitate nature
9. quality of piecing together skillfully; skill at putting forth words or ideas clearly

Beauty is in the Eye
(or Ear) of the Beholder

     If <u>something created by putting pieces together skillfully</u> is obvious--for example, a painting of a flower--it does not require <u>a skillful person</u> who is <u>able to piece words together skillfully</u> to describe it. On the other hand, if you are looking at a sculpture with five <u>jointed</u> arms holding a <u>skillfully made object of historical relevance</u>, a person who is <u>not able to piece words together skillfully</u> may not be able to help you "get it."

     Musically <u>talented people</u> communicate more directly, often using their <u>skill</u> to describe feelings and emotions. In fact, a good singer can make a <u>contrived</u> situation seem real. Conversely, a poorly written song, poorly performed, just sits there like an <u>idle or unskillful</u> object.

<u>Fill in the blanks using words from the **art**, **arti**, **ert** family.</u>

1. Some _____ , especially when it is realistic, is very easy to understand.

2. An _____ might be a painter, a musician, a dancer, or a sculptor.

3. A person who can piece words together well is described as _____ .

4. Some paintings have what looks like five arm all _____ among themselves.

5. The arms in such a painting might be holding some _____ from the past.

6. A person who cannot explain things well would be described as _____ .

7. Some _____ use their voices or musical instruments.

8. They use their _____ to express feelings and emotions.

9. A good singer can persuade a listener that an _____ situation is real.

10. Bad paintings or bad musical performances seem like lifeless, _____ objects.

<u>Word Bank</u>

art	articulate	artificial	inarticulate
artful	articulated	artificially	inert
artfulness	articulately	artist	inertness
articles	artifact	artists	unartistic

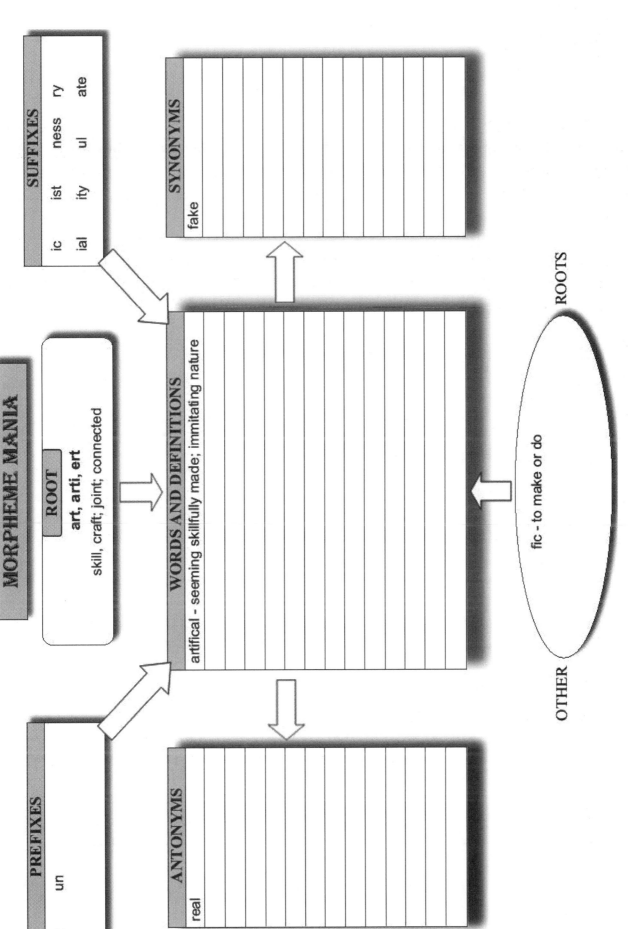

MORPHEME MANIA

PREFIXES
in
un

SUFFIXES
ic   ist   ness   ry
ial   ity   ul   ate

ROOT
art, arti, ert
skill, craft; joint; connected

WORDS AND DEFINITIONS
artifical – seeming skillfully made; immitating nature

SYNONYMS
fake

ANTONYMS
real

ROOTS
fic – to make or do

OTHER

Build as many words as you can for this root family. Use the prefixes and suffixes listed, <u>or add your own</u>. If you use any "combining roots", add them to the "Other Roots" box. Try to think of an antonym and a synonym for each word you build.

www.DynamicLiteracy.com

©2007 Dynamic Literacy, LLC

115

My Word Wall

Root: *art, arti, ert*

Word	Synonym / Antonym	Word	Synonym / Antonym

Morphemes for this meaning family

Prefixes	Roots	Suffixes

Root Squares

How many words can you make?

Start in any square. Your goal is to combine two or more word parts to make as many words in the 'sum, sume, sumpt' family as you can. Write each word and a definition you can think of for it in the space provided at the bottom of the page.

re	ion	pre
able	sum, sume, sumpt	con
as	uous	er

_____

_____

_____

_____

_____

_____

_____

_____

Magic Squares

Select the best answer for each of the words in the 'sum, sume, sumpt' family from the numbered definitions. Put the number in the proper space in the Magic Square box. If the total of the numbers is the same both across and down, you have found the magic number!

'sum, sume, sumpt' means to take up, claim

WORDS
A. assumption
B. consumption
C. presumption
D. assume
E. resume
F. resumption
G. consume
H. presume
I. presumptuously

DEFINITIONS
1. to take again; to start up again
2. took for oneself or claimed; believed to be true
3. took up and used completely
4. to take up and use completely
5. the act of taking for oneself or claiming; the act of believing to be true
6. in a manner taking as true beforehand; in a manner taking liberties
7. that which is taken as true beforehand
8. the act of taking again; the act of starting up again
9. act of taking up and using completely
10. taking as true beforehand
11. to take as true beforehand
12. to take for oneself or claim; to believe to be true

Magic Square Box

A.	B.	C.
D.	E.	F.
G.	H.	I.

Magic Number _____

www.dynamicliteracy.com

Stair Steps

Fill in the missing letters of each SUM, SUME, SUMPT
word by using the definitions below.
SUM, SUME, SUMPT means to take up, claim

1.			s	u	m					
2.			s	u	m					
3.				s	u	m				
4.				s	u	m				
5.				s	u	m				
6.			s	u	m	p	t			
7.				s	u	m				
8.				s	u	m	p	t		
9.				s	u	m	p	t		

1. took again; started up again
2. taking for oneself or claiming; believing to be true
3. took up and used completely
4. people who take up and use completely
5. taking as true beforehand
6. the act of taking for oneself or claiming; the act of believing to be true
7. things taken up and used completely
8. act of taking up and using completely
9. taking or considering as true beforehand; taking liberties

A Spat Over a Cheese Question

Elsie and Charlie were exchanging trivia questions. Elsie asked, "What country per capita <u>takes up and uses completely</u> the most cheese?" "I never thought about it," said Charlie. "I <u>took to myself believing</u> it was Wisconsin."

"Wisconsin's not a country, silly. The answer is France. Its <u>act of taking up and using completely</u> of cheese is huge. Each <u>person who takes up and uses</u> eats over 54 pounds of cheese every year.

"I know Wisconsin's not a country," blurted Charlie, <u>taken up and used up completely</u> with anger at Elsie's <u>act of taking as true beforehand</u> that he was stupid. "I was just kidding! You shouldn't <u>take as true beforehand</u> that people are always serious when they say silly things. I'm not playing trivia with you ever again.

"Oh, yes you will. We'll <u>take up again</u> our game when you've calmed down," teased Elsie.

<u>Fill in the blanks using words from the **sum**, **sume**, **sumpt** family.</u>

1. Charlie is challenged to name the country that presently _____ the most cheese.

2. Making a joke, Charlie said that he _____ that it was one of the U.S. states.

3. The per-capita _____ of cheese is greatest in France.

4. Each _____ of cheese eats about 54 pounds a year.

5. Charlie's anger _____ him to the point that he quit the game.

6. Elsie's comment sounded like a _____ that she was smarter than Charlie.

7. Charlie felt that Elsie should not _____ that he was being serious.

8. Elsie knows Charlie's love of trivia and knows that the game will _____ before too long.

<u>Word Bank</u>

assumed	consumed	consumption	presumptuous
assumption	consumer	presume	resume
consumable	consumes	presumption	resumptions

www.dynamicliteracy.com

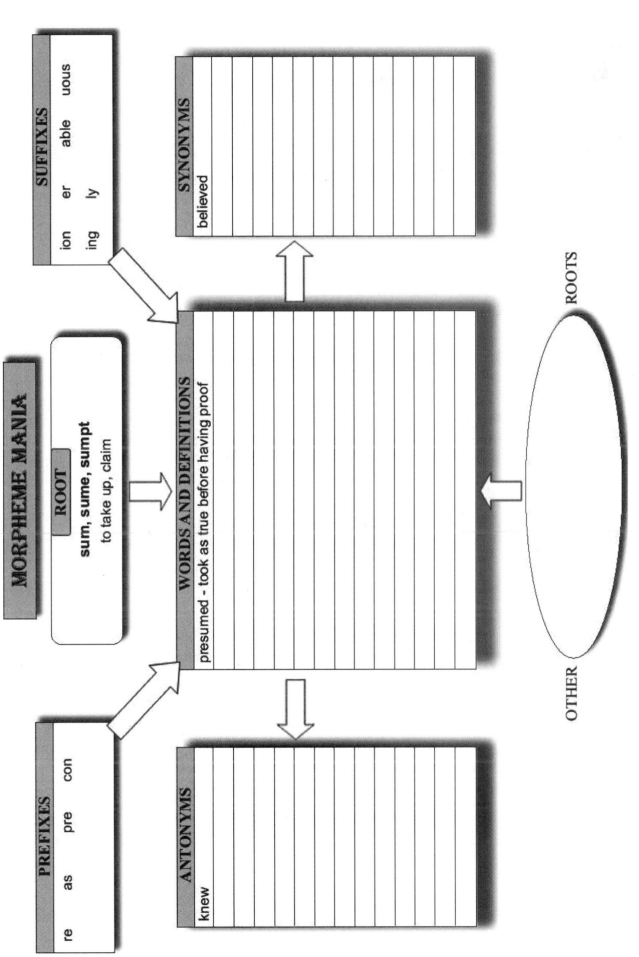

MORPHEME MANIA

PREFIXES
re	as
pre	con

SUFFIXES
ion	er	able	uous
ing	ly		

ROOT
sum, sume, sumpt
to take up, claim

WORDS AND DEFINITIONS
presumed – took as true before having proof

SYNONYMS
believed

ANTONYMS
knew

ROOTS

OTHER

Build as many words as you can for this root family. Use the prefixes and suffixes listed, or add your own. If you use any "combining roots", add them to the "Other Roots" box. Try to think of an antonym and a synonym for each word you build.

www.DynamicLiteracy.com

Root: *sum, sume, sumpt*

Word	Synonym / Antonym	Word	Synonym / Antonym

Morphemes for this meaning family

Prefixes	Roots	Suffixes

Root Squares

How many words can you make?

Start in any square. Your goal is to combine two or more word parts to make as many words in the 'tang, tag, ting, tig, tact' family as you can. Write each word and a definition you can think of for it in the space provided at the bottom of the page.

ent	in	ly
ibil	tang, tag, ting, tig, tact	ful
ious	ial	con

_____

_____

_____

_____

_____

_____

_____

_____

Magic Squares

Select the best answer for each of the words in the 'tang, tag, ting, tig, tact' family from the numbered definitions. Put the number in the proper space in the Magic Square box. If the total of the numbers is the same both across and down, you have found the magic number!

'tang, tag, ting, tig, tact' means to touch, feel, perceive

WORDS	DEFINITIONS
A. contact	1. pertaining to the sense of touch
B. contagion	2. to touch together; to notify
C. contiguous	3. quality of lacking the right touch; lack of poise and diplomacy; rudeness
D. contingent	4. not touched; whole or unbroken
E. intangibly	5. things touching only at a single point
F. intact	6. touching together; depending upon
G. tactful	7. touching together
H. tactlessness	8. in a manner not touched by the senses; abstractly
I. tangents	9. anything transmitted by touching together; a spreading disease
	10. having just the right "touch"; having poise and diplomacy in dealing with others

Magic Square Box

A.	B.	C.
D.	E.	F.
G.	H.	I.

Magic Number ____

www.dynamicliteracy.com

Stair Steps

Fill in the missing letters of each TANG, TAG, TING, TIG, TACT
word by using the definitions below.
TANG, TAG, TING, TIG, TACT means to touch, feel, perceive

1. | | | t | a | c | t |
2. | t | a | c | t | | |
3. | t | a | n | g | | |
4. | | | t | a | c | t |
5. | | t | a | n | g | |
6. | t | a | c | t | | |
7. | t | a | n | g | | |
8. | | | t | i | n | g |
9. | | | t | a | g | |

1. not touched; whole or unbroken
2. having just the right "touch"; having poise and diplomacy in dealing with others
3. able to be perceived by the touch
4. touched together; notified
5. in a manner not touched by the senses; abstractly
6. quality of having the right touch; poise and diplomacy in a situation
7. in a manner touching only slightly
8. acts of touching together; acts of being dependent upon
9. quality of spreading by touching together

Watch That Touch!

In some years, the flu epidemic spreads to all 48 <u>touching</u> states. Some types of flu are very <u>much spread by touching</u>, and it takes only a slight connection <u>pertaining to touch</u> with someone who has the flu for the <u>spread of the disease by touching</u> to occur. Sometime you have to be <u>diplomatic with the right touch</u> and excuse yourself from shaking hands. You may be required by certain <u>required acts that touch together</u>, like handling germy doorknobs, to make physical <u>act of touching together</u> with surfaces that have some potent <u>feature of spreading by touching</u> on them. To keep your health <u>untouched or unbroken</u>, wash your hands frequently. Limiting the epidemic is <u>depending</u> upon everyone being respectful of others.

<u>Fill in the blanks using words from the **tang, tag, ting, tig, tact** family.</u>

1. The 48 states that touch as a group are the _____ states.

2. Diseases spread by touching infected people or surfaces are called _____.

3. The sense of touch is your _____ sense.

4. Quickly-spreading disease is called a _____.

5. Not to appear rude, you sometime have to be _____ and avoid shaking hands.

6. Certain _____ happen to arise where you cannot avoid touching a germy surface, such as when you need to open a door.

7. If you do have to make _____ with a germy surface, wash your hands quickly.

8. The _____ of some diseases is very powerful and quick.

9. Try to be alert in order to keep your health _____.

10. Limiting an epidemic is _____ upon everyone's respectful behavior.

<u>Word Bank</u>

contact	contagiousness	contingent	intangible	tangibly
contagion	contiguous	intact	tactful	tactlessness
contagious	contingencies	intangible	tactile	tangential

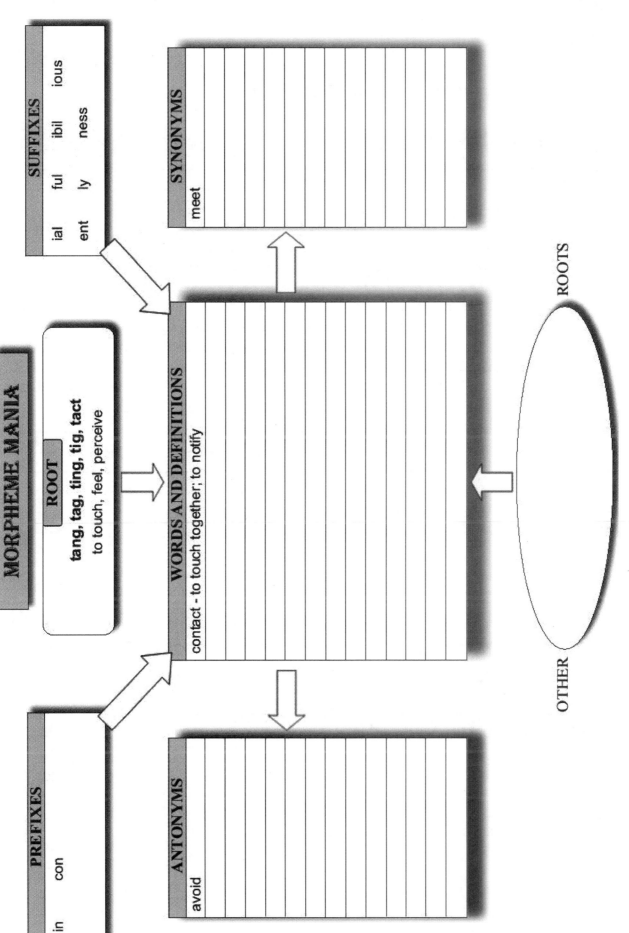

MORPHEME MANIA

PREFIXES
in   con

ROOT
tang, tag, ting, tig, tact
to touch, feel, perceive

SUFFIXES
ial   ful   ibil   ious
ent   ly   ness

WORDS AND DEFINITIONS
contact – to touch together; to notify

SYNONYMS
meet

ANTONYMS
avoid

OTHER ROOTS

Build as many words as you can for this root family. Use the prefixes and suffixes listed, or add your own. If you use any "combining roots", add them to the "Other Roots" box. Try to think of an antonym and a synonym for each word you build.

www.DynamicLiteracy.com

Root: *tang, tag, ting, tig, tact*

Word	Synonym / Antonym	Word	Synonym / Antonym

Morphemes for this meaning family

Prefixes	Roots	Suffixes

Root Squares

How many words can you make?

Start in any square. Your goal is to combine two or more word parts to make as many words in the 'bio, b, bi, be' family as you can. Write each word and a definition you can think of for it in the space provided at the bottom of the page.

sis	on	micro
otic	bio, b, bi, be	ic
graph	sym	y

_____

_____

_____

_____

_____

_____

_____

Magic Squares

Select the best answer for each of the words in the 'bio, b, bi, be' family from the numbered definitions. Put the number in the proper space in the Magic Square box. If the total of the numbers is the same both across and down, you have found the magic number!

'bio, b, bi, be' means life

<table>
<tr><td>WORDS</td><td>DEFINITIONS</td></tr>
<tr><td>A. aerobic</td><td>1. pertaining to the written story of a person's life</td></tr>
<tr><td>B. anaerobic</td><td>2. a person who writes the story of another's life</td></tr>
<tr><td>C. antibiotics</td><td>3. closely associated different species of life</td></tr>
<tr><td>D. autobiographer</td><td>4. a person who specializes in the study of life</td></tr>
<tr><td>E. biographic</td><td>5. substances against living organisms; medicines that destroy germs</td></tr>
<tr><td>F. biopsy</td><td>6. a small living organism</td></tr>
<tr><td>G. microbe</td><td>7. living in air; related to oxygen consumption</td></tr>
<tr><td>H. anaerobes</td><td>8. a person writing about the life of himself or herself</td></tr>
<tr><td>I. biologist</td><td>9. living without air</td></tr>
<tr><td></td><td>10. acting like a life force; a life form enhanced with electronics</td></tr>
<tr><td></td><td>11. organisms that thrive without air</td></tr>
<tr><td></td><td>12. removal and examination of living tissue</td></tr>
</table>

Magic Square Box

A.	B.	C.
D.	E.	F.
G.	H.	I.

Magic Number ____

www.dynamicliteracy.com

Stair Steps

Fill in the missing letters of each BIO, B, BI, BE
word by using the definitions below.
BIO, B, BI, BE means life

1. | b | i | | | | |
2. | | | | | b | e |
3. | | | | | b | e |
4. | | | | b | i | o |
5. | b | i | o | | | |
6. | | | | b | i | |
7. | b | i | o | | | |
8. | b | i | o | | | |
9. | | | | b | i | o |

1. having to do with life
2. a small living organism
3. small living organisms
4. state of living with another; mutual benefit of different species together
5. people who specialize in the study of life
6. substances against living organisms; medicines that destroy germs
7. in a manner relating to the study of life
8. able to go down to basic living parts; able to decay organically
9. related to writing about oneself's life

It's about Life

Whether he or she studies tiny <u>little living organisms</u> that are visible under a microscope or the <u>collective life forms</u> of a desert, a <u>person who studies life</u> is wild about life. These scientists do not of course all study the same kinds of life. Some seek how to protect people from bacteria by creating new <u>substances against living organisms</u>. Others investigate how to make trash <u>capable of being broken down by life forces</u> and less filling for waste sites. Still others examine the <u>state of living together</u> that exists between one organism and another, such as mistletoe and the oak.

It may sound futuristic but there are even some scientists who invent ways to enhance life with electronic arms or legs. Have you ever heard of the <u>life form enhanced with electronics</u> woman or man? Even exercise coaches study life: some exercises, such as running, can be <u>using air in a certain way</u> while others, like lifting weights, are <u>without using air in the same way</u>. It all depends on how oxygen is used.

You don't have to be a scientist to be wild about life. <u>People who write about lives</u> study life, too. From information <u>related to what is written about a life</u> and anecdotes presented in books, readers can gain insight into someone's character.

<u>Fill in the blanks using words from the **bio, b, bi, be** family.</u>

1. Very tiny living things are called _____.

2. All the life forms of a particular region, such as a desert, are together called the _____ of that region.

3. A _____ studies all forms of living things.

4. _____ such as penicillin kill bacteria or other harmful life forms.

5. Waste-site owners prefer garbage to be _____.

6. Two organisms that are interdependent show _____, a relationship that helps each other to live.

7. Medicine combined with technology created _____ arms and legs.

8. Running is _____ exercise while weight lifting is _____.

9. _____ write about the lives of other people.

10. Authors use _____ data from family members to write about a famous person's life.

<u>Word Bank</u>

aerobic	biodegradable	biographies	biopsy	microbes
anaerobic	biographers	biologist	bioscientific	symbiosis
antibiotics	biographical	bionic	biota	symbiotic

www.dynamicliteracy.com

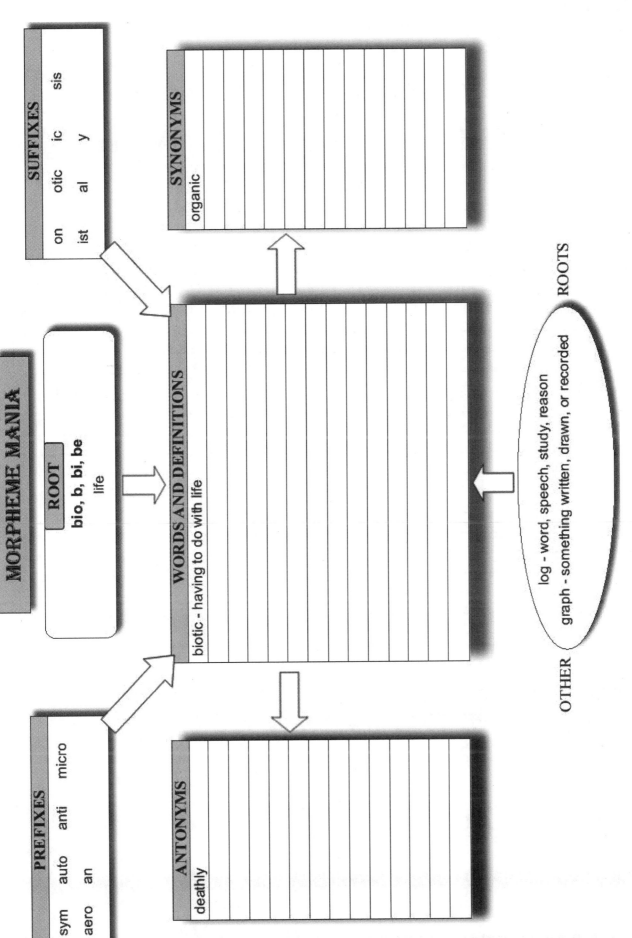

MORPHEME MANIA

PREFIXES

sym	auto	anti	micro
aero	an		

ROOT

bio, b, bi, be

life

SUFFIXES

on	otic	ic	sis
ist	al	y	

WORDS AND DEFINITIONS

biotic – having to do with life

SYNONYMS

organic

ANTONYMS

deathly

OTHER ROOTS

log – word, speech, study, reason

graph – something written, drawn, or recorded

Build as many words as you can for this root family. Use the prefixes and suffixes listed, or add your own. If you use any "combining roots", add them to the "Other Roots" box. Try to think of an antonym and a synonym for each word you build.

www.DynamicLiteracy.com

Root: *bio, b, bi, be*

Word	Synonym / Antonym	Word	Synonym / Antonym

Morphemes for this meaning family

Prefixes	Roots	Suffixes

Root Squares

How many words can you make?

Start in any square. Your goal is to combine two or more word parts to make as many words in the 'nomin, nomen, nom' family as you can. Write each word and a definition you can think of for it in the space provided at the bottom of the page.

ee	ive	s
de	nomin, nomen, nom	ion
ate	poly	ial

_____

_____

_____

_____

_____

_____

_____

Magic Squares

Select the best answer for each of the words in the 'nomin, nomen, nom' family from the numbered definitions. Put the number in the proper space in the Magic Square box. If the total of the numbers is the same both across and down, you have found the magic number!

'nomin, nomen, nom' means name

WORDS	DEFINITIONS
A. binomial	1. involving religious groups of different names
B. denominator	2. that which puts a name or value down; the number below the line of a fraction
C. ignominious	3. consisting of many names or terms
D. nomenclature	4. related to a name; a word in the subjective case
E. ignomy	5. consisting of three names or three terms
F. nominative	6. quality of not having a reputable name
G. polynomial	7. having two names or two terms
H. renominate	8. a system to call things by name
I. trinomial	9. marked by shame and dishonor on a name
	10. to name again for an office or award

Magic Square Box

A.	B.	C.
D.	E.	F.
G.	H.	I.

Magic Number ____

www.dynamicliteracy.com

Stair Steps

Fill in the missing letters of each NOMIN, NOMEN, NOM, NOMO word by using the definitions below.

NOMIN, NOMEN, NOM, NOMO means name

1. | | | n | o | m | | |
2. | n | o | m | i | n | |
3. | | n | o | m | | |
4. | | | n | o | m | |
5. | n | o | m | i | n | |
6. | | | n | o | m | |
7. | n | o | m | e | n | |
8. | | n | o | m | i | n | |
9. | | n | o | m | i | n | |

1. quality of not having a reputable name
2. a person named for an office or award
3. having two names or two terms
4. consisting of three names or three terms
5. a naming for an office or award
6. math sentences with many names or terms
7. a system to call things by name
8. acts of naming again for an office or award
9. related to a group named after someone or something

137

The Name and Fame of Caesar

Like most upper-class Romans, Caesar's name was <u>consisting of three names</u>. Most people know him by his identity <u>consisting of two names</u>, Julius Caesar, but actually his full <u>system of name calling</u> was Gaius Julius Caesar. Most people thought that he should be awarded in some special way for all that he had done for Rome. Therefore, he was <u>named for an office</u> to hold life-long absolute power, but he refused at first. After he was <u>named again for an office</u>, he accepted. This <u>act of naming for an office</u> caused some friends to turn against him. As the <u>person named to an office</u> for dictator, he tried to assure people that he would use his power for the good of the country, and would not bring <u>a shameful dishonorable name</u> to Rome. He said that he would only <u>in name</u> be a dictator but would rule like a regular consul by consulting advisers and the Senate. Some friends, however, thought that the very acceptance of a life term of power was <u>marked by shame and dishonor on a name</u> and they determined that he had to be stopped.

Fill in the blanks using words from the **nomin, nomen, nom, nomo** family:

1. Most upper class Romans' names were _____.

2. Caesar is more familiar to us by his _____ name.

3. The full _____ of Caesar was Gaius Julius Caesar.

4. A majority of people _____ Caesar to be dictator for life.

5. Refusing the first time, Caesar was _____ by the people.

6. His _____ as life-long dictator alarmed some Romans.

7. Caesar as _____ tried to assure everyone that he would be a good ruler.

8. He said he would not bring shame and _____ to the Roman Republic.

9. Caesar declared that he would be a dictator _____, but in reality he would be a regular consul, or executive officer.

10. A few Romans felt that it was _____ of Caesar even to accept the power.

<u>Word Bank</u>

binomial	ignominy	nomination	nominees
denominations	nomenclature	nominatively	renominated
ignominious	nominated	nominee	trinomial

www.dynamicliteracy.com

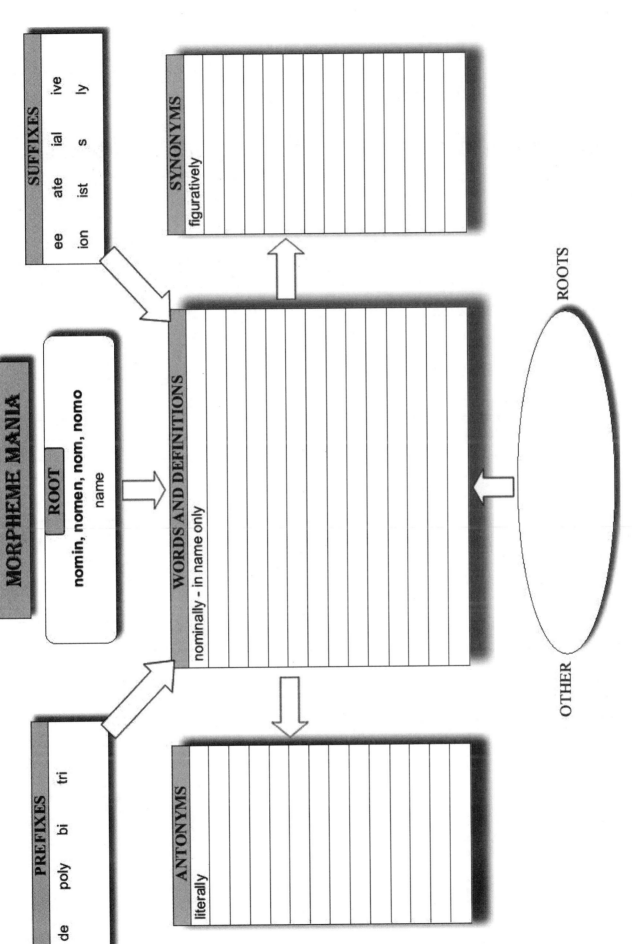

MORPHEME MANIA

PREFIXES
de
poly   bi
tri

ROOT
nomin, nomen, nom, nomo
name

SUFFIXES
ee   ate   ial   ive
ion   ist   s   ly

WORDS AND DEFINITIONS
nominally – in name only

SYNONYMS
figuratively

ANTONYMS
literally

ROOTS

OTHER

Build as many words as you can for this root family. Use the prefixes and suffixes listed, or add your own. If you use any "combining roots", add them to the "Other Roots" box. Try to think of an antonym and a synonym for each word you build.

www.DynamicLiteracy.com

Root: *nomin, nomen, nom, nomo*

Word	Synonym / Antonym	Word	Synonym / Antonym

Morphemes for this meaning family

Prefixes	Roots	Suffixes

Root Squares

How many words can you make?

Start in any square. Your goal is to combine two or more word parts to make as many words in the 'ordin, ord' family as you can. Write each word and a definition you can think of for it in the space provided at the bottom of the page.

sub	ary	extra
ate	ordin, ord	ance
ly	or	co

_____

_____

_____

_____

_____

_____

_____

_____

Magic Squares

Select the best answer for each of the words in the 'ordin, ord' family from the numbered definitions. Put the number in the proper space in the Magic Square box. If the total of the numbers is the same both across and down, you have found the magic number!

'ordin, ord' means row, rank, arrangement

WORDS	DEFINITIONS
A. coordinate	1. logical arrangement of things
B. disordered	2. a person who arranges together; a person who makes things harmonious
C. disorderly	3. of a specific rank in a numbered arrangement
D. extraordinary	4. being in the first rank; early, basic
E. insubordinate	5. not having arrangement; messy
F. order	6. in accord with normal arrangements; typically
G. ordinarily	7. to arrange together; to make harmonious
H. primordial	8. beyond the expected arrangement; remarkable
I. subordinate	9. in a manner lacking arrangement; in an unorganized manner
	10. of common rank or arrangement; commonly encountered; usual
	11. to put in a lower rank
	12. not behaving in one's lower rank; defiant against authority

Magic Square Box

A.	B.	C.
D.	E.	F.
G.	H.	I.

Magic Number _____

www.dynamicliteracy.com

Stair Steps

Fill in the missing letters of each ORDIN, ORD
word by using the definitions below.
ORDIN, ORD means row, rank, arrangement

1.	o	r	d	i	n			
2.				o	r	d		
3.				o	r	d		
4.			o	r	d	i	n	
5.				o	r	d		
6.			o	r	d	i	n	
7.			o	r	d	i	n	
8.			o	r	d	i	n	
9.				o	r	d	i	n

1. of common rank or arrangement; commonly encountered; usual
2. situations lacking arrangement; messy conditions
3. in a manner lacking arrangement; in an unorganized manner
4. arranges together; makes harmonious
5. causing to be out of arrangement; causing to be unorganized
6. in a manner not arranged in a regular way
7. acts of arranging together; acts of making harmonious
8. putting in a lower rank
9. in a manner beyond expected arrangement; remarkable

 The Spartans

The ancient Spartans led a very <u>neatly-arranged</u> life, almost like <u>early-rank</u> bees or ants. There was an intentional <u>arrangement in the same pattern</u> of dress, education, and military service. To outsiders of <u>common rank or arrangement</u>, Spartans seemed to have a devotion <u>not arranged in usual pattern</u> to their state. Everything personal was <u>put in a lower rank</u> to the state. Spartans were trained to endure harsh conditions <u>in a manner beyond expected arrangement</u> such as extreme cold and hunger. They tolerated no <u>disturbed arrangement</u> in their routines, and any acts of disobedience and <u>qualities of not behaving in one's lower rank</u> were punished severely. This group <u>beyond the expected arrangement</u> of people once very famously <u>arranged together</u> a failed but valiant defense against Greek enemies. This story was told in the film *300*.

<u>Fill in the blanks using words from the **ordin**, **ord** family.</u>

1. The life of the ancient Spartans was very _____.

2. They lived almost like the _____ lives of bees or other social insects.

3. There was a careful _____ of social customs and habits.

4. They did not consider themselves _____ Greeks, but as a special people.

5. Other Greeks thought that their love of country was _____.

6. Personal matters were _____ to matters of the state.

7. Spartans trained themselves to endure _____ harsh situations.

8. A society like that of the Spartans tolerated no _____ in their routines.

9. Acts of_____ were dealt with in a severe manner.

10. The Spartan struggle against their enemies was _____.

11. They _____ an effort that failed but brought glory anyway.

<u>Word Bank</u>

coordinated	extraordinarily	order	ordinary
coordination	extraordinary	orderly	primordial
disorder	inordinate	ordinal	subordinated
disorderly	insubordination	ordinances	subordination

www.dynamicliteracy.com

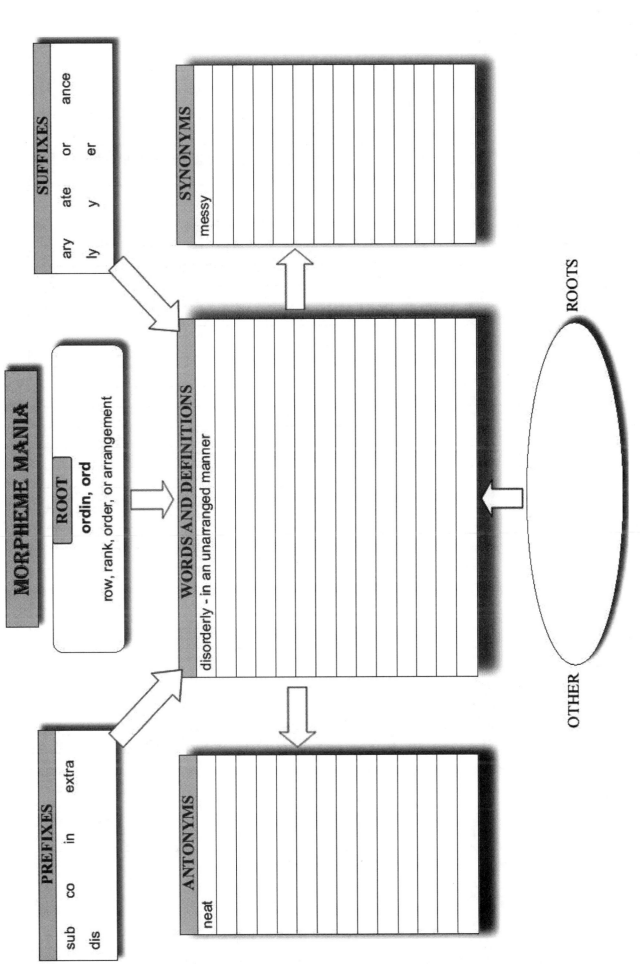

MORPHEME MANIA

PREFIXES

sub	co	in	extra
dis			

ROOT

ordin, ord

row, rank, order, or arrangement

SUFFIXES

ary	ate	or	ance
ly	y	er	

WORDS AND DEFINITIONS

disorderly - in an unarranged manner

SYNONYMS

messy

ANTONYMS

neat

ROOTS

OTHER

Build as many words as you can for this root family. Use the prefixes and suffixes listed, or add your own. If you use any "combining roots", add them to the "Other Roots" box. Try to think of an antonym and a synonym for each word you build.

www.DynamicLiteracy.com

My Word Wall

Name

Root: *ordin, ord*

Word	Synonym / Antonym	Word	Synonym / Antonym

Morphemes for this meaning family

Prefixes	Roots	Suffixes

Root Squares

How many words can you make?

Start in any square. Your goal is to combine two or more word parts to make as many words in the 'centr, center, centri' family as you can. Write each word and a definition you can think of for it in the space provided at the bottom of the page.

ec	ize	al
anthropo	centr, center, centri	ic
ate	con	ity

_____

_____

_____

_____

_____

_____

_____

_____

Magic Squares

Select the best answer for each of the words in the 'centr, center, centri' family from the numbered definitions. Put the number in the proper space in the Magic Square box. If the total of the numbers is the same both across and down, you have found the magic number!

'centr, center, centri' means center, middle, ordinary

WORDS	DEFINITIONS
A. anthropocentric	1. having a common middle
B. central	2. driving away from the middle
C. centrifugal	3. related to the earth being the middle
D. concentrate	4. to remove from the middle; to remove from one authority
E. decentralize	5. quality of putting oneself in the middle; an act of self-importance
F. eccentric	6. out of the middle; odd
G. geocentric	7. placing humans in the middle; explaining everything in human terms
H. egocentricity	8. to focus attention on the middle
I. center	9. at or near the middle
	10. at greatest distance from outside points; middle

Magic Square Box

A.	B.	C.
D.	E.	F.
G.	H.	I.

Magic Number ____

Stair Steps

Fill in the missing letters of each CENTR, CENTER, CENTRI
word by using the definitions below.
CENTR, CENTER, CENTRI means center, middle, ordinary

1. | c | e | n | t | r |
2. | c | e | n | t | e | r |
3. | | | c | e | n | t | r |
4. | | | | c | e | n | t | r | i | c |
5. | c | e | n | t | r | i |
6. | | | c | e | n | t | r |
7. | | | c | e | n | t | r |
8. | c | e | n | t | r |
9. | | | | | | | | c | e | n | t | r |

1. at or near the middle
2. placed in the middle
3. out of the middle; odd
4. related to the earth being the middle
5. driving away from the middle
6. to remove from the middle; to remove from one authority
7. focusing attention on the middle
8. a bringing to or near the middle
9. placing humans in the middle; explaining everything in human terms

At the Morphics Bee

The local <u>odd, out of the middle</u> Paige Turner was master of ceremonies of the Morphics Bee. One of his <u>behaviors out of he middle</u> was that he would dress up as a bee at this particular event. He sat in the <u>middle</u> of the room in a revolving chair and called out morphemes from his location <u>at or near the middle</u> to the contestants, who were arranged in circles <u>having a common middle</u> around him. Even though he had a seat <u>brought to or near the middle</u>, he had <u>removed</u> the game <u>from the middle</u> by having a scorer located at each contestant's side. The contestants would <u>focus attention on the middle</u> very hard and give their answers to their own scorekeeper, who would then carry the scores to Mr. Turner in his seat located <u>so as to be at or near the middle</u>.

<u>Fill in the blanks using words from the **centr**, **center**, **centri** family.</u>

1. Paige Turner was an _____ man who did strange, harmless things.

2. One of his _____ was to dress up like a bee at the Morphemes Bee.

3. He would sit in the _____ of the room calling out morphemes.

4. In his _____ location, he would move around in a revolving chair.

5. The contestants were arranged in _____ circles around him.

6. He had _____ his position in the room.

7. Score keeping was completely _____, with scorers all over the place.

8. Contestants had to _____ hard to get their answers right.

9. Scores would be brought to Mr. Turner in his _____ located seat.

<u>Word Bank</u>

anthropocentric	centralizations	centrifugal	decentralized
center	centralized	concentrate	eccentric
central	centrally	concentric	eccentricities

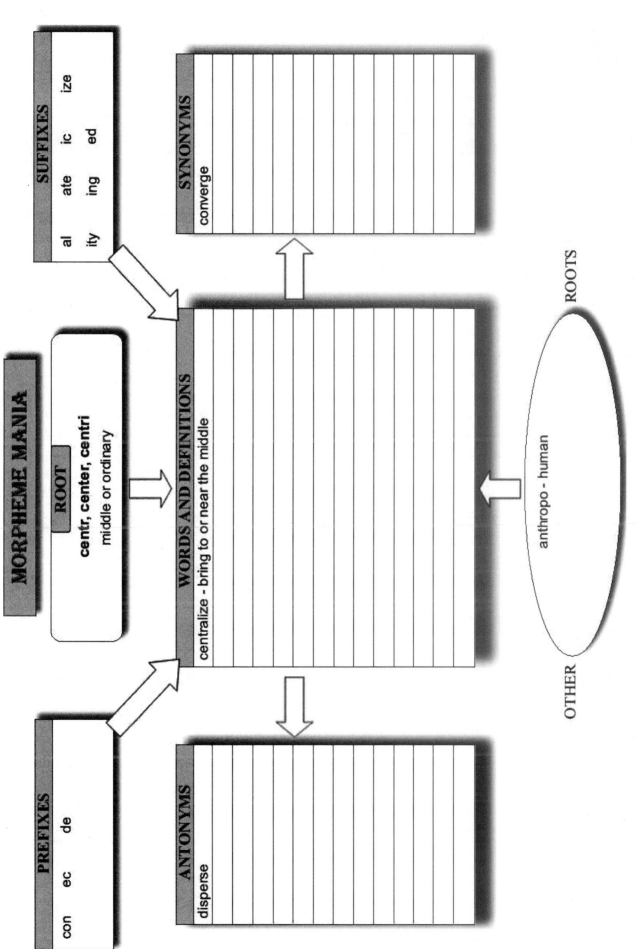

MORPHEME MANIA

PREFIXES

con   ec   de

SUFFIXES

al   ate   ic   ize

ity   ing   ed

ROOT

centr, center, centri

middle or ordinary

WORDS AND DEFINITIONS

centralize - bring to or near the middle

SYNONYMS

converge

ANTONYMS

disperse

OTHER ROOTS

anthropo - human

Build as many words as you can for this root family. Use the prefixes and suffixes listed, or <u>add your own</u>. If you use any "combining roots", add them to the "Other Roots" box. Try to think of an antonym and a synonym for each word you build.

151

Root: *centr, center, centri*

Word	Synonym / Antonym	Word	Synonym / Antonym

Morphemes for this meaning family

Prefixes	Roots	Suffixes

Root Squares

How many words can you make?

Start in any square. Your goal is to combine two or more word parts to make as many words in the 'cycl, cycle, cyclo' family as you can. Write each word and a definition you can think of for it in the space provided at the bottom of the page.

one	bi	ing
ist	cycl, cycle, cyclo	re
ic	tri	ed

_____

_____

_____

_____

_____

_____

_____

_____

Magic Squares

Select the best answer for each of the words in the 'cycl, cycle, cyclo' family from the numbered definitions. Put the number in the proper space in the Magic Square box. If the total of the numbers is the same both across and down, you have found the magic number!

'cycl, cycle, cyclo' means circle or wheel

WORDS	DEFINITIONS
A. bicyclists	1. riding a three-wheeled vehicle
B. cyclical	2. a mythological circle-eyed giant
C. cyclones	3. a book for teaching a wide circle of topics
D. motorcycle	4. circled around again; reused
E. motorcycled	5. people who ride two-wheeled vehicles
F. tricycling	6. periods in which events come around in circles
G. recycled	7. occurring in predictable circles of time
H. cycles	8. rode an open, wheeled vehicle moved by an engine
I. motorcyclers	9. violent circling windstorms
	10. showing a wide circle of knowledge
	11. people who ride wheeled vehicles moved by an engine
	12. an open, wheeled vehicle moved by an engine

Magic Square Box

A.	B.	C.
D.	E.	F.
G.	H.	I.

Magic Number ____

www.dynamicliteracy.com

Stair Steps

Fill in the missing letters of each CYCL, CYCLE, CYCLO
word by using the definitions below.
CYCL, CYCLE, CYCLO means circle or wheel

1.	c	y	c	l						
2.	c	y	c	l						
3.			c	y	c	l	e			
4.			c	y	c	l	e			
5.	c	y	c	l						
6.		c	y	c	l					
7.					c	y	c	l		
8.		c	y	c	l	o				
9.				c	y	c	l			

1. came around in a circle of time
2. a violent circling windstorm
3. two-wheeled vehicles
4. circles around again; reuses
5. mythological circle-eyed giants
6. people who ride two-wheeled vehicles
7. rode an open, wheeled vehicle moved by an engine
8. showing a wide circle of knowledge
9. people who ride wheeled vehicles moved by an engine

If you can pedal a vehicle, you can assist a good cause. During the early fall, <u>people who pedal two-wheeled vehicles</u>, <u>people who pedal three-wheeled vehicles</u>, and even <u>people who pedal one-wheeled vehicles</u> hop aboard their choice way to ride and log miles for charity. Only <u>open engine-driven vehicles</u> are not allowed in these races that use only leg power. <u>Pedaling wheeled vehicles</u> up and down hills and over smooth and rough terrain, the travelers consume gallons of water from <u>reused, circled around</u> plastic bottles as they speed around curves, churning up leaves in a <u>circling windstorm</u> as they pass.

Once the <u>circular repeated period</u> of races is over in the late fall, a team is named the best fundraiser for the season. Their picture is printed in the newspaper, and, if the total money raised is quite large, their picture might even appear in a <u>book for teaching a wide circle of topics</u> of world records. But, don't worry about the <u>people who ride open engine-driven vehicles</u>. They have their own races.

<u>Fill in the blanks with words from the **cycl**, **cycle**, **cyclo** family.</u>

1. _____ pedal vehicles with two wheels, _____ use three
   wheels, and _____ travel on vehicles with one wheel.

2. Motored vehicles such as cars or _____ are forbidden in races for
   pedal-operated vehicles.

3. Riding with no help from a motor is the sport of _____.

4. Plastic bottles can be _____ into other products.

5. A _____ of swirling leaf follows the racers.

6. Each year there is a new _____ of a few different races.

7. Recorded in an _____ of world records are the data from the races.

8. _____ have their own category of races to win.

<u>Word Bank</u>

bicyclers	cycling	encyclopedia	motorcyclists	tricyclers
cycle	cyclone	motorcycle	recycled	unicyclers
cyclical	cyclops	motorcycles	recycling	unicycling

www.dynamicliteracy.com

156

MORPHEME MANIA

PREFIXES

en re bi tri

ROOT

cycl, cycle, cyclo

circle or wheel

SUFFIXES

ia one er ist
ed ing al ic

WORDS AND DEFINITIONS

cyclical - occuring in predictable circles of time

SYNONYMS

recurring

ANTONYMS

single

OTHER ROOTS

ped - child; related to teaching
ops - sight, eye, view; observation

Build as many words as you can for this root family. Use the prefixes and suffixes listed, or add your own. If you use any "combining roots", add them to the "Other Roots" box. Try to think of an antonym and a synonym for each word you build.

www.DynamicLiteracy.com

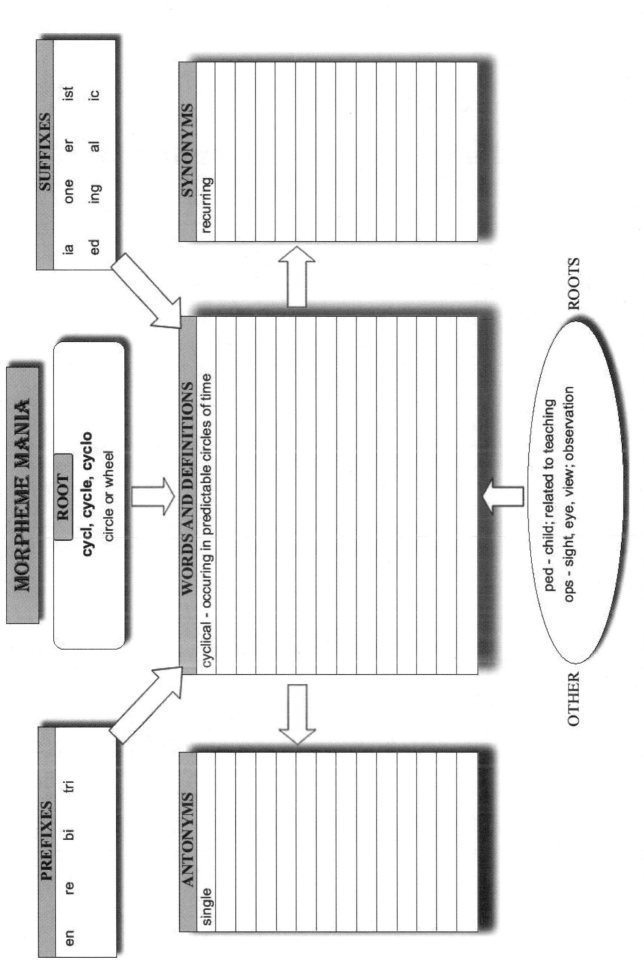

My Word Wall

Name

Root: *cycl, cycle, cyclo*

Word	Synonym / Antonym	Word	Synonym / Antonym

Morphemes for this meaning family

Prefixes	Roots	Suffixes

Root Squares

How many words can you make?

Start in any square. Your goal is to combine two or more word parts to make as many words in the 'migr' family as you can. Write each word and a definition you can think of for it in the space provided at the bottom of the page.

ion	ory	non
im	migr	trans
e	ate	ant

_____

_____

_____

_____

_____

_____

_____

_____

Magic Squares

Select the best answer for each of the words in the 'migr' family from the numbered definitions. Put the number in the proper space in the Magic Square box. If the total of the numbers is the same both across and down, you have found the magic number!

'migr' means to move

WORDS	DEFINITIONS
A. emigrant	1. a person who moves; a person who undergoes periodic relocation
B. emigrate	2. to move out; to relocate to another country
C. emigration	3. moved in; moved into a country from another
D. immigrating	4. moving in; moving into a country from another
E. migrants	5. related to moving from one region to another
F. migrate	6. people moving; people traveling around a country seeking work
G. migrational	7. act of moving out; act of leaving one's country for another
H. transmigrate	8. to move; to relocate periodically
I. immigrated	9. a person moving out; a person leaving his or her country for another
	10. to move across; to pass through one place on the way to another

Magic Square Box

A.	B.	C.
D.	E.	F.
G.	H.	I.

Magic Number ____

www.dynamicliteracy.com

Stair Steps

Fill in the missing letters of each MIGR
word by using the definitions below.
MIGR means to move

1.	m	i	g	r									
2.	m	i	g	r									
3.	m	i	g	r									
4.	m	i	g	r									
5.		m	i	g	r								
6.			m	i	g	r							
7.			m	i	g	r							
8.			m	i	g	r							
9.						m	i	g	r				

1. to move; to relocate periodically
2. moves; relocates periodically
3. the act of moving; the act of relocating periodically
4. undergoing movement; undergoing periodic relocation
5. act of moving out; act of leaving one's country for another
6. moving in; moving into a country from another
7. acts of moving in; acts of relocating people into a country
8. pertaining to the act of moving in; related to moving into a country
9. movement across; passage through one place on the way to another

"You lazy goose," the others in the flock honked at Guinevere when they passed her walking south. "We're <u>moving</u> and you should be, too."

"I AM. My <u>act of moving</u> is just slower. I'm tired of being a seasonal <u>person moving</u>, anyway. Fly south; fly north. Back and forth, back and forth. All this <u>moving out</u> and <u>moving in</u> is wearing out my wings, not to mention my sense of humor," she honked back. "For once, I'd like to put these <u>seasonal paths of periodic movement</u> on hold and stay put for a whole year." And so she did. Guinevere learned to knit little goose sweaters for the cold and fashioned boots from forest debris. In the dark winter days she wrote her memoirs, *Why I Don't <u>Relocate Periodically</u>*.

<u>Specialists in patterns of movement</u> hailed the book as a groundbreaking revelation into animal psychology. Guinevere made millions. And, yes, these days she is <u>likely to undergo movement</u>: Miami Beach in a limo.

<u>Fill in the blanks with words from the **migr** family</u>.

1. The geese were _____ south.

2. Guinevere's _____ was slower than her goose pals'.

3. Tired of being a seasonal _____, Guinevere wanted to stay put.

4. She was tired of _____ out of one habitat and _____ into a different one.

5. Guinevere did not like the flock's many seasonal _____.

6. Her memoirs were about her decision not to _____.

7. _____ who study migrating birds were amazed by the book.

8. As a rich goose in a limo headed for Florida, Guinevere is _____ once again.

<u>Word Bank</u>

emigrant	immigrational	migrating	migratories
emigrating	migrant	migration	migratory
immigrated	migrate	migrationists	nonimmigrant
immigrating	migrated	migratory	

www.dynamicliteracy.com

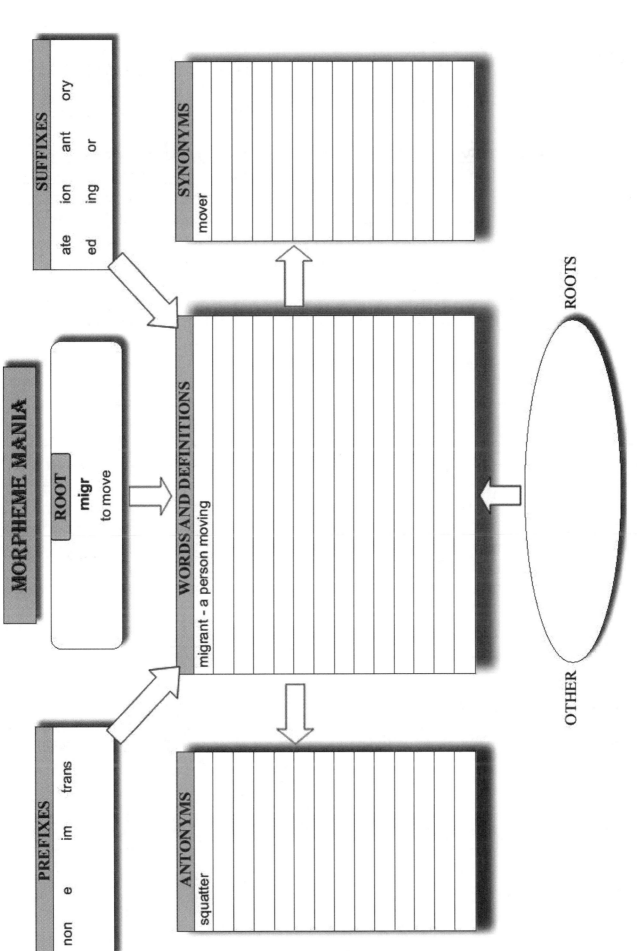

MORPHEME MANIA

PREFIXES

non	e
im	trans

SUFFIXES

ate	ion	ant	ory
ed	ing	or	

ROOT

migr
to move

WORDS AND DEFINITIONS

migrant – a person moving

SYNONYMS

mover

ANTONYMS

squatter

ROOTS

OTHER

Build as many words as you can for this root family. Use the prefixes and suffixes listed, or add your own. If you use any "combining roots", add them to the "Other Roots" box. Try to think of an antonym and a synonym for each word you build.

www.DynamicLiteracy.com

Root: *migr*

Word	Synonym / Antonym	Word	Synonym / Antonym

Morphemes for this meaning family

Prefixes	Roots	Suffixes

Root Squares

How many words can you make?

Start in any square. Your goal is to combine two or more word parts to make as many words in the 'don, done, dat, date' family as you can. Write each word and a definition you can think of for it in the space provided at the bottom of the page.

par	ing	able
ate	don, done, dat, date	or
ion	con	s

_____

_____

_____

_____

_____

_____

_____

_____

Magic Squares

Select the best answer for each of the words in the 'don, done, dat, date' family from the numbered definitions. Put the number in the proper space in the Magic Square box. If the total of the numbers is the same both across and down, you have found the magic number!

'don, done, dat, date' means to give

WORDS
A. condone
B. condoners
C. data
D. dated
E. datum
F. donation
G. pardonable
H. pardoned
I. postdated

DEFINITIONS
1. a given fact
2. able to give a time or time period for
3. a person who gives; a person who presents to a worthy cause
4. able to be given completely; capable of being excused or relieved from penalty
5. to give thoroughly; to allow or overlook a misdeed
6. wrote a given time later than now
7. things given; pieces of information
8. something given; a presentation to a worthy cause
9. people who give thoroughly; people who allow or overlook misdeeds
10. gave; presented to a worthy cause
11. gave completely; excused or relieved from penalty
12. gave a time or time period to

Magic Square Box

A.	B.	C.
D.	E.	F.
G.	H.	I.

Magic Number ____

www.dynamicliteracy.com

Stair Steps

Fill in the missing letters of each DON, DONE, DAT, DATE
word by using the definitions below.
DON, DONE, DAT, DATE means to give

1. | d | a | t | |
2. | d | a | t | |
3. | d | a | t | |
4. | d | o | n | |
5. | d | a | t | |
6. | | | d | o | n | e |
7. | d | o | n | |
8. | | | d | a | t | |
9. | | | d | o | n | |

1. things given; pieces of information
2. a given fact
3. pertaining to giving
4. people who give; people giving to worthy causes
5. able to give a time or time period for
6. gives thoroughly; allows or overlooks a misdeed
7. people who give; people who present to worthy causes
8. wrote a given time later than now
9. able to be given completely; capable of being excused or relieved
   from penalty

Forgiving Fines

When Wilmer and Wilda Pennywise succeeded in their writing careers, they <u>gave</u> much of their wealth to their local public library. The library staff was happy with the money from such generous <u>people who give</u> and planned a banquet in celebration of the <u>presentation to a worthy cause</u>.

While checking names in the <u>given information</u> about library patrons for the guest list, a library worker noticed that the Pennywises owed many overdue fines. It was also discovered that the Pennywises had lost several volumes over the years. Holding a celebration for such patrons would appear to be <u>overlooking a misdeed</u> for such careless behavior.

The staff notified the Pennywises, who were embarrassed and said they would be <u>giving</u> new editions of the lost books and more money to make up for the fines. They had simply lost track of the <u>given points in time</u> that the books were due.

The Pennywises requested that the library have a policy once a year of <u>giving release from</u> penalty to forgetful people if they returned or bought new books. And so, every March 24, the library <u>gives release from penalty</u> for fines for the day if the books are returned.

<u>Fill in the blanks with words from the **don, done, dat, date** family.</u>

1. The Pennywises _____ money to the public library.

2. The generous _____ were to be honored with a celebration.

3. Their _____ to the library was large.

4. A staff member checked past _____ about library users.

5. The staff didn't want to seem to be _____ careless, forgetful behavior.

6. To make up for their mistakes, the authors would be _____ new books and even more money.

7. The authors had just not paid enough attention to the _____ that the books had been due.

8. From then on, the library would be _____ forgetful people once a year.

9. Every March 24, the library _____ fines if late books are returned.

Word Bank

condone	condoning	dated	donation	pardoned
condoner	data	dates	donating	pardoning
condoners	datable	donated	donors	pardons

www.dynamicliteracy.com

MORPHEME MANIA

PREFIXES

par   con

ROOT

don, done, dat, date

to give

SUFFIXES

ate   ion   able   s

a   ing   or

WORDS AND DEFINITIONS

donor - a person who gives

SYNONYMS

giver

ANTONYMS

recipient

ROOTS

OTHER

Build as many words as you can for this root family. Use the prefixes and suffixes listed, or add your own. If you use any "combining roots", add them to the "Other Roots" box. Try to think of an antonym and a synonym for each word you build.

www.DynamicLiteracy.com

169

My Word Wall

Name

Root: *don, done, dat, date*

Word	Synonym / Antonym	Word	Synonym / Antonym

Morphemes for this meaning family

Prefixes	Roots	Suffixes

Root Squares

How many words can you make?

Start in any square. Your goal is to combine two or more word parts to make as many words in the 'cid, cide, cis, cise' family as you can. Write each word and a definition you can think of for it in the space provided at the bottom of the page.

in	homi	ive
de	**cid, cide, cis, cise**	ex
ion	pre	ness

_____

_____

_____

_____

_____

_____

_____

_____

Magic Squares

Select the best answer for each of the words in the 'cid, cide, cis, cise' family from the numbered definitions. Put the number in the proper space in the Magic Square box. If the total of the numbers is the same both across and down, you have found the magic number!

'cid, cide, cis, cise' means to cut; kill or cut down

WORDS	DEFINITIONS
A. decidedly	1. an act of killing a member of mankind
B. decisiveness	2. the act of cutting out; removal, usually by surgery
C. excision	3. thoroughly and cleanly cut; exact
D. homicidal	4. related to killing a member of mankind
E. incisions	5. agent that kills animals with incut bodies; bug poison
F. indecisive	6. not quick to select or cut out from; not choosing quickly
G. insecticide	7. quality of being quick to cut out from; the ability to make quick choices
H. precise	8. acts of cutting in; surgical cuts into bodily tissue
I. precision	9. in a manner selected or cut out from; so as to be chosen from a set of possibilities
	10. quality of being thoroughly and cleanly cut; exactness

Magic Square Box

A.	B.	C.
D.	E.	F.
G.	H.	I.

Magic Number _____

Stair Steps

Fill in the missing letters of each CID, CIDE, CIS, CISE
word by using the definitions below.
CID, CIDE, CIS, CISE means to cut; kill or cut down

1.			c	i	d		
2.				c	i	s	e
3.			c	i	s		
4.				c	i	d	e
5.				c	i	d	
6.			c	i	s		
7.			c	i	s	e	
8.					c	i	d	e
9.			c	i	s		

1. selected or cut out from; chose from a set of possibilities
2. thoroughly and cleanly cut; exact
3. a cutting in; a surgical cut into bodily tissue
4. an act of killing a ruler or king
5. related to killing a member of mankind
6. in a manner tending to cut into; sharply and penetratingly
7. quality of cutting thoroughly and cleanly; quality of being exact
8. agents that kill animals with incut bodies; bug poisons
9. quality of not being quick to cut out from; inability to make quick choices

Crime Scene Detective

After scolding Rhett for spraying a whole can of <u>bug killer</u> on a mound of large, black ants, Roynetta decided to treat the scene as a detective would if investigating the scene of <u>an act of killing a human</u>. Using a sharp stick, Roynetta <u>cut out</u> half of the mound <u>in a manner thoroughly cut</u> down the middle. Marveling at the <u>exactness</u> of the operation, Roynetta began to daydream of being the lead detective on a big case making comments <u>tending to cut into</u>, directing the team with <u>thoroughly clean-cut</u> instructions.

Roynetta's <u>acts of cutting in</u> into the ant mound had exposed the hub of its life: the chamber of the queen. Solving the case with the <u>quality of being thoroughly cut</u> of Sherlock Holmes, Roynetta declared the crime to be one of <u>an act of killing a ruler</u>. The queen was no more. She would charge Rhett with the crime.

<u>Fill in the blanks with words from the **cid**, **cide**, **cis**, **cise** family.</u>

1. Rhett sprayed a can of _____ on a mound of ants.

2. Roynetta treated the killings as a _____ although no humans were involved.

3. She _____ the mound _____ down the middle.

4. Roynetta was amazed at her careful _____ in delving into the mound of ants.

5. She imagines her cutting, _____ comments to her team.

6. Investigating a crime scene requires _____ instructions from the leader.

7. Roynetta's _____ into the mound exposed the queen.

8. She analyzed the situation with the _____ of a detective.

9. _____ was recorded as the crime of killing the queen.

Word Bank

decided	excised	incisive	precise	precision
decisive	homicide	indecisiveness	precisely	regicide
excisions	incisions	insecticide	preciseness	regicidal

www.dynamicliteracy.com

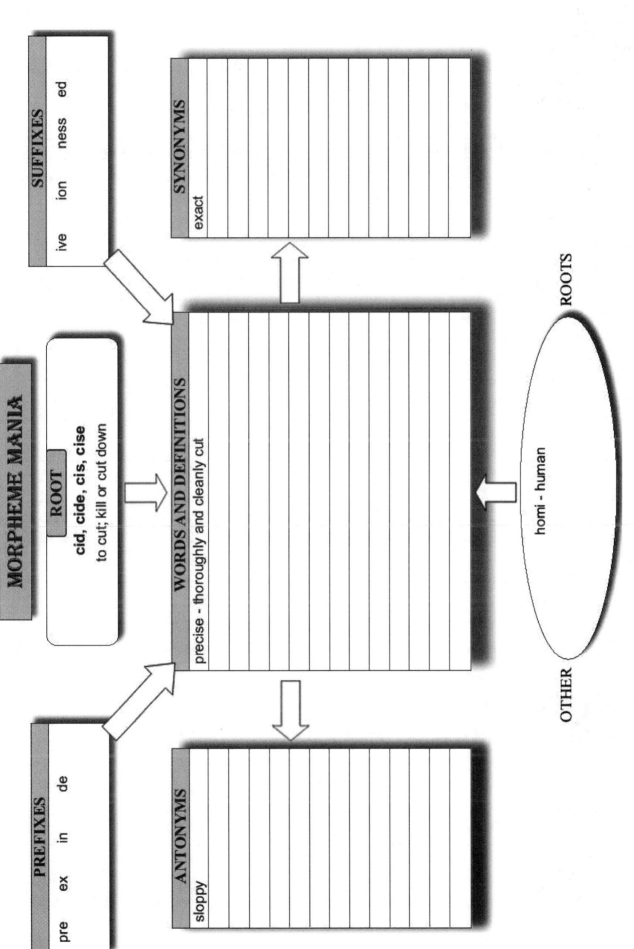

MORPHEME MANIA

PREFIXES
pre   ex   in   de

SUFFIXES
ive   ion   ness   ed

ROOT
cid, cide, cis, cise
to cut; kill or cut down

WORDS AND DEFINITIONS
precise - thoroughly and cleanly cut

SYNONYMS
exact

ANTONYMS
sloppy

ROOTS
OTHER

homi - human

Build as many words as you can for this root family. Use the prefixes and suffixes listed, or add <u>your own</u>. If you use any "combining roots", add them to the "Other Roots" box. Try to think of an antonym and a synonym for each word you build.

www.DynamicLiteracy.com

175

My Word Wall

Root: *cid, cide, cis, cise*

Word	Synonym / Antonym	Word	Synonym / Antonym

Morphemes for this meaning family

Prefixes	Roots	Suffixes

Root Squares

How many words can you make?

Start in any square. Your goal is to combine two or more word parts to make as many words in the 'grav, grave, gravi, griev, grieve, grief' family as you can. Write each word and a definition you can think of for it in the space provided at the bottom of the page.

ate	ance	est
ous	grav, grave, gravi, griev, grieve, grief	ity
ly	er	ag

_____

_____

_____

_____

_____

_____

_____

_____

Magic Squares

Select the best answer for each of the words in the 'grav, grave, gravi, griev, grieve, grief' family from the numbered definitions. Put the number in the proper space in the Magic Square box. If the total of the numbers is the same both across and down, you have found the magic number!

'grav, grave, gravi, griev, grieve, grief' means heavy or weight

WORDS	DEFINITIONS
A. aggravate	1. animals that move heavily
B. grave	2. act of making heavier; act of annoying or of intensifying
C. gravest	3. a declaration of heaviness; a proclamation of sadness or harm done
D. gravigrades	4. in a manner full of heaviness; severely or seriously
E. gravitated	5. heaviest, most serious, most important
F. gravitation	6. the quality of being full of heaviness; severity or seriousness
G. griever	7. heavy, serious, important
H. grievousness	8. moved as if pulled by weight
I. grievously	9. to make heavier; to annoy or to intensify
	10. full of heaviness; severe or serious
	11. a person who feels heaviness; mourner
	12. act or process of being pulled by weight

Magic Square Box

A.	B.	C.
D.	E.	F.
G.	H.	I.

Magic Number ____

www.dynamicliteracy.com

Stair Steps

Fill in the missing letters of each GRAV, GRAVE, GRAVI, GRIEV, GRIEVE, GRIEF word by using the definitions below.

GRAV, GRAVE, GRAVI, GRIEV, GRIEVE, GRIEF means heavy or weight

1. | g | r | a | v | | |
2. | g | r | a | v | e |
3. | g | r | a | v |
4. | g | r | i | e | v |
5. | g | r | a | v |
6. | g | r | i | e | v |
7. | g | r | a | v | i |
8. | | | g | r | a | v |
9. | g | r | a | v |

1. heavier, more serious, more important
2. in a heavy, serious manner
3. state of being heavy; seriousness
4. full of heaviness; severe or serious
5. to move as if pulled by weight
6. in a manner full of heaviness; severely or seriously
7. animals that move heavily
8. acts of making heavier; acts of annoying or of intensifying
9. related to being pulled by weight

179

The Sad Donkey

Poor Donkey Hodey was always <u>feeling heaviness</u> over his lot in life. He <u>felt heaviness</u> about how his owner loaded his back with <u>heavy</u> amounts of stuff. He noticed that the horses didn't have any <u>declarations of heaviness</u> with their owner, who pampered them and fed them nice oats. Donkey Hodey tried to <u>move as if pulled by weight</u> toward the horses' food trough, but they pushed him away. He now understood the <u>seriousness or heaviness</u> of personality that his retired old Uncle Donkey Shane had. The fact that the other animals wouldn't help <u>made heavier or intensified</u> his role as a <u>person who feel heaviness</u>. What a <u>full-of-heaviness</u> life poor, lonely Donkey Hodey led.

<u>Fill in the blanks with words from the **grav**, **grave**, **gravi**, **griev**, **grieve**, **grief** family.</u>

1. The poor donkey was constantly _____ about how hard its life was.

2. Mostly it _____ about having to carry so much weight.

3. Its farmer owner piled _____ amounts of stuff on its back.

4. The horses didn't seem to have any _____ against the farmer.

5. Donkey Hodey would often try to _____ toward the horses' food.

6. He now understood why there was such _____ in his Uncle Donkey Shane's personality.

7. The fact that none of Donkey Hodey's farm colleagues would help _____ his sadness.

8. The poor donkey was just meant to be a _____ in life.

9. It certainly led a _____ life.

<u>Word Bank</u>

aggravated	gravest	grief	griever
aggravations	gravitate	grievances	grieving
grave	gravity	grieved	grievous

MORPHEME MANIA

PREFIXES

ag

ROOT

grav, grave, gravi, griev, grieve, grief
heavy or weight

SUFFIXES

| ance | ate | er | est |
| ity | | ly | ous | ing |

WORDS AND DEFINITIONS

grieving - feeling heaviness or sadness

SYNONYMS

mourning

ANTONYMS

blissful

OTHER ROOTS

Build as many words as you can for this root family. Use the prefixes and suffixes listed, or add your own. If you use any "combining roots", add them to the "Other Roots" box. Try to think of an antonym and a synonym for each word you build.

www.DynamicLiteracy.com

Root: *grav, grave, gravi, griev, grieve, grief*

Word	Synonym / Antonym	Word	Synonym / Antonym

Morphemes for this meaning family

Prefixes	Roots	Suffixes

Root Squares

How many words can you make?

Start in any square. Your goal is to combine two or more word parts to make as many words in the 'viv, vive, vivi, vit' family as you can. Write each word and a definition you can think of for it in the space provided at the bottom of the page.

id	ious	al
ity	viv, vive, vivi, vit	sur
re	ize	ac

_____

_____

_____

_____

_____

_____

_____

_____

Magic Squares

Select the best answer for each of the words in the 'viv, vive, vivi, vit' family from the numbered definitions. Put the number in the proper space in the Magic Square box. If the total of the numbers is the same both across and down, you have found the magic number!

'viv, vive, vivi, vit' means alive, life

WORDS	DEFINITIONS
A. convivial	1. action or state of living beyond or over; state of being alive after a disaster
B. revivalist	2. characterized by enjoyment of life with others; festive and jolly
C. survivors	3. brings to life again; brings out of unconsciousness
D. vividly	4. in a lively manner; so as to be peppy
E. vivaciously	5. making lively again; refreshing
F. vitally	6. in a manner resembling life; brightly and clearly
G. vital	7. people who live beyond or over; people still alive after disasters
H. revitalizing	8. in a manner required for life; necessarily
I. revives	9. a person who brings to life again; a person who leads a meeting to reawaken faith
	10. relating to life; necessary

Magic Square Box

A.	B.	C.
D.	E.	F.
G.	H.	I.

Magic Number ____

www.dynamicliteracy.com

Stair Steps

Fill in the missing letters of each VIV, VIVE, VIVI, VIT word by using the definitions below.

VIV, VIVE, VIVI, VIT means alive, life

1. | v | i | t | | |
2. | | | v | i | v | e |
3. | | | | v | i | v | e |
4. | | | v | i | v | |
5. | v | i | t | | |
6. | | | v | i | v | |
7. | v | i | v | | |
8. | | | v | i | v | |
9. | | | v | i | t | |

1. relating to life; necessary
2. to bring to life again; to bring out of unconsciousness
3. to live beyond or over; to be alive after a disaster
4. bringing to life again; bringing out of unconsciousness
5. quality of being alive; pep or energy
6. people who live beyond or over; people still alive after disasters
7. in a lively manner; so as to be peppy
8. the enjoyment of life with others; quality of being festive and jolly
9. making lively again; refreshing

Loving Life

Many people now live to be over 100 years old. When you look into the faces, <u>characterized by enjoyment of life with others</u>, of these older people, you can see that having a sense of humor and a love of life lends to their <u>quality of being alive</u>. Some after retiring from their jobs have <u>made lively again</u> their existence by volunteering in schools. Reading with the <u>lively, peppy</u> children benefits both the child and volunteer. Indulging a passion is another way <u>to bring to life again</u> a love of existence. Painting, writing, and sharing <u>bright and clear</u> pictures taken on a trip all can add to this love and enjoyment. Many people will be <u>living beyond</u> to very old age for several reasons. Family genes and a <u>living beyond</u> disease are a couple of those factors, but having <u>an enjoyment of live with others</u> of spirit that <u>makes lively again</u> a person's attitude about everything is important. An upbeat attitude may even be the answer to anyone's becoming a <u>person who lives beyond</u>.

<u>Fill in the blanks using words from the **viv, vive, vivi, vit** family.</u>

1. Happy people, no matter how old, have _____ faces.

2. Love of life leads to _____.

3. Volunteering has _____ many people's lives after retirement.

4. Most _____ children enjoy having someone with whom to read.

5. There are many ways to _____ a love of life.

6. Colorful, _____ photos help in remembering a trip.

7. Many people will be experience _____ many years.

8. Family history is one factor for a _____ to old age.

9. Happy _____ of spirit leads to an upbeat attitude.

10. A good attitude _____ many as they get older.

11. Becoming a _____ may depend on a good attitude.

<u>Word Bank</u>

convivial	revitalizes	survive	vital	vivaciously
conviviality	revive	surviving	vitality	vivid
revitalized	survival	survivor	vivacious	vividly

www.dynamicliteracy.com

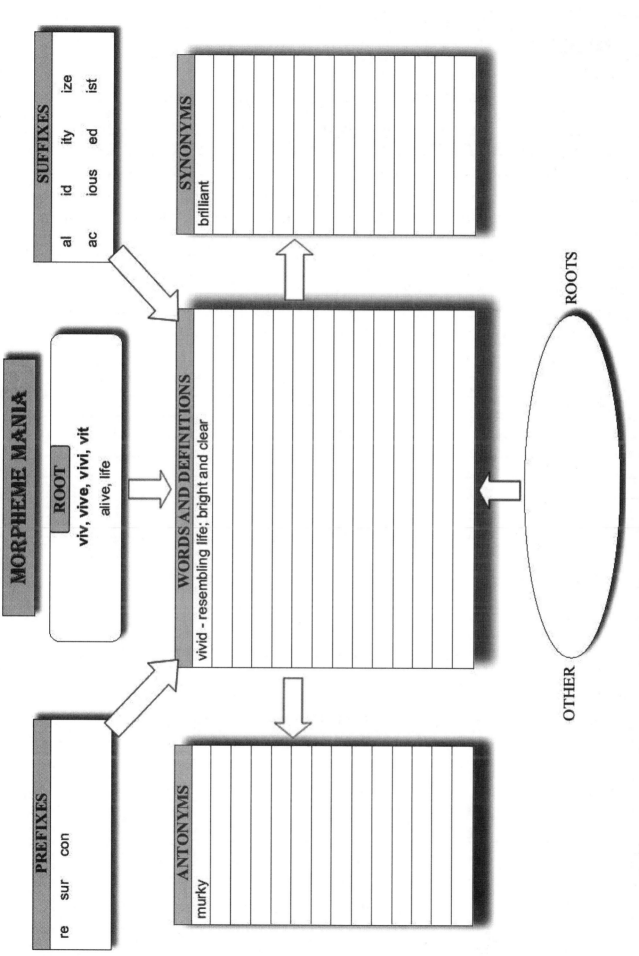

MORPHEME MANIA

PREFIXES

re   sur   con

SUFFIXES

al   id   ity   ize
ac   ious   ed   ist

ROOT

viv, vive, vivi, vit

alive, life

WORDS AND DEFINITIONS

vivid – resembling life; bright and clear

SYNONYMS

brilliant

ANTONYMS

murky

OTHER ROOTS

Build as many words as you can for this root family. Use the prefixes and suffixes listed, or add your own. If you use any "combining roots", add them to the "Other Roots" box. Try to think of an antonym and a synonym for each word you build.

www.DynamicLiteracy.com

187

My Word Wall

Name

Root: *viv, vive, vivi, vit*

Word	Synonym / Antonym	Word	Synonym / Antonym

Morphemes for this meaning family

Prefixes	Roots	Suffixes

Root Squares

How many words can you make?

Start in any square. Your goal is to combine two or more word parts to make as many words in the 'sequ, secu, secut, secute' family as you can. Write each word and a definition you can think of for it in the space provided at the bottom of the page.

el	con	ion
per	sequ, secu, secut, secute	sub
ent	ence	ial

_____

_____

_____

_____

_____

_____

_____

_____

_____

Magic Squares

Select the best answer for each of the words in the 'sequ, secu, secut, secute' family from the numbered definitions. Put the number in the proper space in the Magic Square box. If the total of the numbers is the same both across and down, you have found the magic number!

'sequ, secu, secut, secute' means to follow

WORDS

A. consecutive
B. consecutively
C. consequences
D. inconsequential
E. persecute
F. prosecutes
G. sequel
H. sequence
I. subsequent

DEFINITIONS

1. not following along with; having no results
2. characterized by an action that follows with; serving as a result
3. characterized by following; in linear pattern
4. a series that follows; an orderly progression
5. in a manner following along with; so as to be in a row
6. following after or beneath; coming as a result
7. actions that follow along with; results
8. follows forward; pursues in court
9. following along with; in a row
10. act of following forward; act of pursuing in court
11. something that follows; a continuation or follow-up
12. to follow after thoroughly; to hunt down and harass

Magic Square Box

A.	B.	C.
D.	E.	F.
G.	H.	I.

Magic Number ____

www.dynamicliteracy.com

Stair Steps

Fill in the missing letters of each SEQU, SECU, SECUT, SECUTE
word by using the definitions below.

SEQU, SECU, SECUT, SECUTE means to follow

1. | s | e | q | u | | |

2. | s | e | q | u | | | |

3. | | | s | e | c | u | t | e |

4. | | | s | e | q | u | |

5. | | | s | e | c | u | t |

6. | | | s | e | q | u | |

7. | | | s | e | c | u | t |

8. | | | s | e | c | u | t |

9. | | | | s | e | q | u | | | |

1. something that follows; a continuation or follow-up
2. a series that follows; an orderly progression
3. to follow forward; to pursue in court
4. following after or beneath; coming as a result
5. act of following forward; act of pursuing in court
6. in the manner likely to follow along with; as a result
7. acts of following after thoroughly; acts of hunting down and harassing
8. in a manner following along with; so as to be in a row
9. not following along with; having no results

The Value of Myth

Ancient people wanted to understand why things happened as they did. They didn't have scientific knowledge to explain what happened; <u>as a following result</u>, they told stories. A story might explain the <u>orderly progression</u> of the seasons while a <u>continuation or follow-up</u> to that story might explain why a certain season was so cold. Another story might explain the phases <u>in a row</u> of the moon as they passed <u>in a manner characterized by following</u> throughout a number of days. Stories <u>following after</u> may have delved into the history of the moon goddess herself or even her <u>act of being followed thoroughly after</u> by the god that ruled the day as he banished her to the night.

Another use for the stories was to instruct people as to how to live. The <u>acts that follow along</u> for disobeying the gods would be harsh. The gods may <u>follow after thoroughly</u> the wicked by utterly destroying their lives. Rather than being entertainment <u>with no results</u>, ancient stories explained the mysteries of life and taught proper behavior.

<u>Fill in the blanks using words from the</u> **sequ, secu, secut, secute** <u>family</u>.

1. Early peoples did not have adequate scientific knowledge for natural events. _____ they made up stories to explain them.

2. The seasons form a _____ of changes in weather.

3. A _____ to one story may become an account of a god or goddess.

4. Phases of the moon form a _____ pattern each month.

5. The phases of the moon follow _____ from new moon to new moon.

6. After one story about a goddess, _____ ones may tell more of her behavior.

7. Some gods underwent _____ by more powerful gods.

8. Disobeying a god would result in harsh _____.

9. The gods would _____ people who did not obey their rules.

10. In ancient days these stories were not _____ tales but teaching tools

Word Bank

consecutive	inconsequential	prosecuted	sequences
consequences	persecute	sequel	sequentially
consequently	persecution	sequence	subsequent

www.dynamicliteracy.com

MORPHEME MANIA

PREFIXES

per	sub	con	in
pro			

SUFFIXES

el	ent	ial	ion
ly	ence	ive	

ROOT

sequ, secu, secut, secute

to follow

WORDS AND DEFINITIONS

consecutive – following along with, in a row

SYNONYMS

serial

ANTONYMS

random

ROOTS

OTHER

Build as many words as you can for this root family. Use the prefixes and suffixes listed, or add your own. If you use any "combining roots", add them to the "Other Roots" box. Try to think of an antonym and a synonym for each word you build.

193

Root: *sequ, secu, secut, secute*

Word	Synonym / Antonym	Word	Synonym / Antonym

Morphemes for this meaning family

Prefixes	Roots	Suffixes

Root Squares

How many words can you make?

Start in any square. Your goal is to combine two or more word parts to make as many words in the 'greg' family as you can. Write each word and a definition you can think of for it in the space provided at the bottom of the page.

con	ed	se
de	greg	ion
ag	al	ate

_____

_____

_____

_____

_____

_____

_____

_____

Magic Squares

Select the best answer for each of the words in the 'greg' family from the numbered definitions. Put the number in the proper space in the Magic Square box. If the total of the numbers is the same both across and down, you have found the magic number!

'greg' means flock, group

WORDS	DEFINITIONS
A. aggregation	1. gathered together into a group; assembled
B. congregation	2. tending to flock into a group; friendly and sociable
C. desegregation	3. a group gathered together; act of compiling or amassing
D. segregation	4. the process of moving apart into separate groups; act or process of establishing group divisions
E. gregarious	5. process of grouping back together after separation; act or process of removing group divisions
F. aggregated	6. having been grouped back together after separation; removed group divisions
G. segregated	
H. desegregated	7. a group gathered together; an assembled group
I. congregated	8. moved apart into separate groups; established group divisions
	9. caused to gather together into a group; compiled or amassed

Magic Square Box

A.	B.	C.
D.	E.	F.
G.	H.	I.

Magic Number ____

Stair Steps

Fill in the missing letters of each GREG
word by using the definitions below.
GREG means to flock, group

		g	r	e	g						
1.											
2.	g	r	e	g							
3.			g	r	e	g					
4.		g	r	e	g						
5.			g	r	e	g					
6.		g	r	e	g						
7.		g	r	e	g						

1. to move apart into separate groups; to establish group divisions
2. tending to flock into a group; friendly and sociable
3. gathered together into a group; assembled
4. groups gathered together; acts of compiling or amassing
5. moving back together from separate groups; removing group divisions
6. pertaining to a group gathered together; relating to an assembled group
7. believers in moving apart into separate groups; people advocating establishing group divisions

Students Flock to Make New Friends

Students at Goshen School, just as at most schools, are creatures highly friendly and sociable, <u>tending to flock into a group</u>, but in the past they would <u>move themselves apart into separate groups</u> and <u>gather into a group together</u> in familiar places with familiar people. The <u>grouped mass</u> of upper-grade students seemed to meet in the courtyard after school. A <u>group gathered toward each other</u> of middle-level students met on the track. Lower-level classmates held their <u>grouping together</u> in the cafeteria, afraid to wander into the territory of the other classes.

All that has changed this year. During the new student orientation in September, Goshen upper-class students decided that they would encourage a <u>process of grouping back</u> by class and mingle with the newcomers to make them feel more welcome. Now the lower-class students feel more comfortable and the upper-class students have made new friends.

<u>Fill in the blanks using words from the **greg** family.</u>

1. Students are _____: they always enjoy getting together and talking.

2. Sometime students _____ themselves by gender or age.

3. People who are alike in some way tend to _____ together into the same places.

4. An _____ mass of people all alike used to meet in the courtyard.

5. An _____ of the middle-level students used to meet on the track.

6. Lower-levels seemed forced to have their _____ in the cafeteria.

7. Student-led _____ has made everybody feel more comfortable and friendlier.

<u>Word Bank</u>

aggregated	congregational	desegregating	gregariously
aggregating	congregate	desegregation	segregate
aggregation	congregation	gregarious	segregationists

www.dynamicliteracy.com

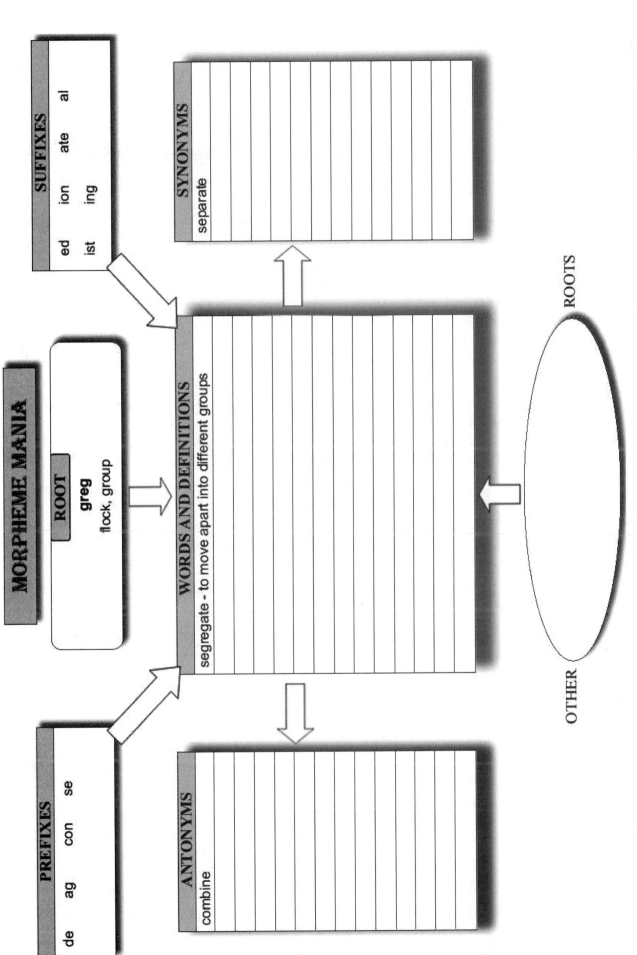

MORPHEME MANIA

PREFIXES
de	ag	con	se

SUFFIXES
ed	ion	ate	al
ist	ing		

ROOT
greg
flock, group

WORDS AND DEFINITIONS
segregate - to move apart into different groups

SYNONYMS
separate

ANTONYMS
combine

OTHER
ROOTS

Build as many words as you can for this root family. Use the prefixes and suffixes listed, or add your own. If you use any "combining roots", add them to the "Other Roots" box. Try to think of an antonym and a synonym for each word you build.

All rights reserved

www.DynamicLiteracy.com

199

Root: *greg*

Word	Synonym / Antonym	Word	Synonym / Antonym

Morphemes for this meaning family

Prefixes	Roots	Suffixes

Root Squares

How many words can you make?

Start in any square. Your goal is to combine two or more word parts to make as many words in the 'sacr, sacra, sacri, sacro, secr' family as you can. Write each word and a definition you can think of for it in the space provided at the bottom of the page.

de	ial	ment
fice	sacr, sacra, sacri, sacro, secr	lege
ate	ed	con

_____

_____

_____

_____

_____

_____

_____

_____

Magic Squares

Select the best answer for each of the words in the 'sacr, sacra, sacri, sacro, secr' family from the numbered definitions. Put the number in the proper space in the Magic Square box. If the total of the numbers is the same both across and down, you have found the magic number!

'sacr, sacra, sacri, sacro, secr' means holy, revered

WORDS

A. consecrate
B. desecrate
C. desecration
D. sacrament
E. sacramental
F. sacred
G. sacrificial
H. sacrileges
I. sacrilegious

DEFINITIONS

1. a person who takes away the holiness of; a person who dishonors or blasphemes
2. to make completely holy; to bless or sanctify
3. acts of depriving things of their holy character; acts of blasphemy or dishonor
4. holy
5. tending to deprive something of its holy character; showing blasphemy or dishonor
6. something holy; a religious rite or symbol
7. act of taking away the holiness of; act of dishonoring or blaspheming
8. concerning something holy; relating to a religious rite or symbol
9. to take away the holiness of; to dishonor or blaspheme
10. relating to what is made holy; serving to give up as an offering something revered

Magic Square Box

A.	B.	C.
D.	E.	F.
G.	H.	I.

Magic Number _____

Stair Steps

Fill in the missing letters of each SACR, SACRA, SACRI, SACRO, SECR word by using the definitions below.

SACR, SACRA, SACRI, SACRO, SECR means holy, revered

1.	s	a	c	r						
2.	s	a	c	r	i					
3.			s	e	c	r				
4.			s	e	c	r				
5.				s	e	c	r			
6.			s	e	c	r				
7.	s	a	c	r	a					
8.	s	a	c	r	i					

1. in a holy manner
2. to make holy; to give up as an offering something revered
3. a person who takes away the holiness of; a person who dishonors or blasphemes
4. taking away the holiness of; dishonoring or blaspheming
5. making completely holy; blessing or sanctifying
6. acts of taking away the holiness of; acts of dishonoring or blaspheming
7. in a manner concerning holy things; so as to relate to a religious rite or symbol
8. so as to deprive something of its holy character; in a manner showing blasphemy or dishonor

A Ceremony is Almost Ruined

The Athenians were celebrating a sacred holiday in honor of their national goddess, Athena. They were <u>consecrating</u> a new temple to her and <u>sacrificing</u> a calf in her honor. One of the <u>sacraments</u> of the ceremony, a robe <u>consecrated</u> to Athena, was being carried in a parade. A priest noticed that someone <u>desecrated</u> the robe by stepping on it. It would be a <u>sacrilege</u> to offer such a robe, so a new one had to be made quickly. Even though the <u>desecration</u> had been an accident, the <u>desecrator</u> had acted <u>sacrilegiously</u> and had to provide an additional <u>sacrificial</u> calf.

<u>Fill in the blanks using words from the **sacr**, **sacra**, **sacri**, **sacro**, **secr** family</u>.

1. This particular day was a _____ day in honor of Athena.

2. The Athenians were _____ a new temple.

3. They were also _____ a calf to the goddess.

4. One of the _____ of the ceremony was a holy robe.

5. The robe was holy because it had been _____ to the goddess Athena.

6. Someone in the crowd stepped on the robe and _____ it.

7. To present a soiled robe to Athena would be a _____.

8. The _____ of the robe had not been intentional.

9. The person who was the _____ of the robe probably felt terrible.

10. That person surely had not meant to act _____.

11. The guilty person had to provide another _____ calf for the goddess.

<u>Word Bank</u>

consecrate	desecrated	sacraments	sacrificing
consecrated	desecration	sacred	sacrilege
consecrating	desecrator	sacrificial	sacrilegiously

www.dynamicliteracy.com

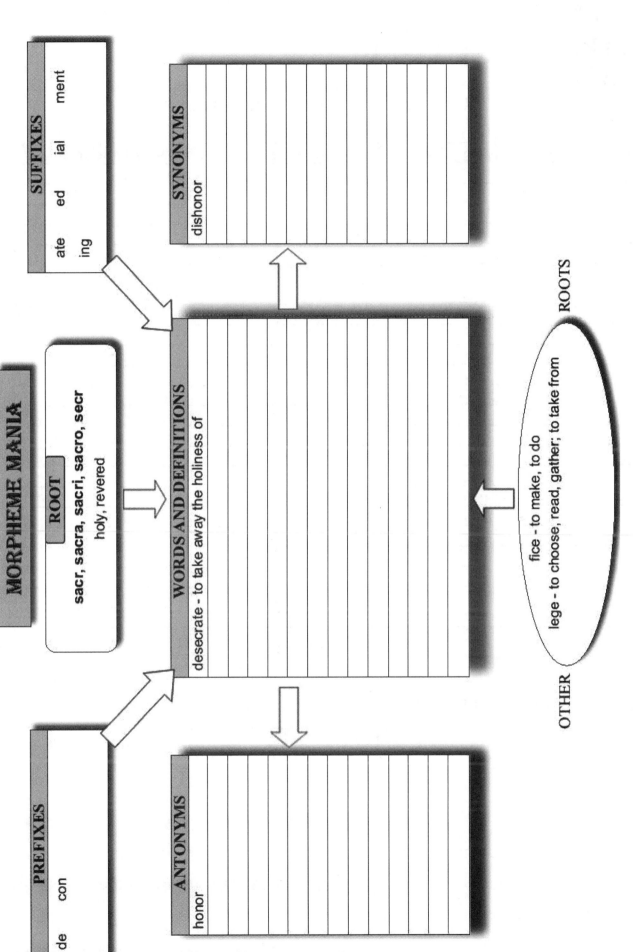

MORPHEME MANIA

PREFIXES

de	con

ROOT

sacr, sacra, sacri, sacro, secr

holy, revered

SUFFIXES

ate	ed	ial	ment
ing			

WORDS AND DEFINITIONS

desecrate – to take away the holiness of

SYNONYMS

dishonor

ANTONYMS

honor

OTHER ROOTS

fice – to make, to do

lege – to choose, read, gather; to take from

Build as many words as you can for this root family. Use the prefixes and suffixes listed, or add your own. If you use any "combining roots", add them to the "Other Roots" box. Try to think of an antonym and a synonym for each word you build.

www.DynamicLiteracy.com

My Word Wall

Name

Root: *sacr, sacra, sacri, sacro, secr*

Word	Synonym / Antonym	Word	Synonym / Antonym

Morphemes for this meaning family

Prefixes	Roots	Suffixes

Root Squares

How many words can you make?

Start in any square. Your goal is to combine two or more word parts to make as many words in the 'lud, lude, lus' family as you can. Write each word and a definition you can think of for it in the space provided at the bottom of the page.

pre	ive	dis
ion	lud, lude, lus	al
il	e	de

_____

_____

_____

_____

_____

_____

_____

_____

Magic Squares

Select the best answer for each of the words in the 'lud, lude, lus' family from the numbered definitions. Put the number in the proper space in the Magic Square box. If the total of the numbers is the same both across and down, you have found the magic number!

'lud, lude, lus' means play, mock, or be deceitful

WORDS	DEFINITIONS
A. preludes	1. performance or event played after all other parts
B. interlude	2. in a manner deceiving away from; so as to sneak by or get around
C. illusion	3. to mock away from; to mislead from the truth
D. elusively	4. mockeries or deceptions in the mind; false perceptions
E. eluding	5. playfully makes reference to; suggests or intimates
F. disillusioned	6. a mockery or deception in the mind; a false perception
G. deluded	7. playful references to; acts of suggesting or intimating
H. allusions	8. performance or event played in between parts
I. alludes	9. deceiving away from; sneaking by or getting around
	10. performances or events played before other parts
	11. to make playful reference to; to suggest or intimate
	12. mocked away from; misled from the truth
	13. took away a mockery or deception in the mind

Magic Square Box

A.	B.	C.
D.	E.	F.
G.	H.	I.

Magic Number ____

Stair Steps

Fill in the missing letters of each LUD, LUDE, LUS
word by using the definitions below.
LUD, LUDE, LUS means to play, mock, or be deceitful

1.   l u d e
2.   l u d e
3.   l u s
4.   l u d
5.   l u s
6.   l u d e
7.   l u s
8.   l u s

1. to deceive away from; to sneak by or get around
2. to make playful reference to; to suggest or imitate
3. tending to deceive away from; tending to sneak by or get around
4. mocking away from; misleading from the truth
5. playful references to; acts of suggesting or imitating
6. performances or events played in between parts
7. act of taking away a mockery or deception in the mind
8. acts of taking away mockeries or deceptions in the mind

Disappointment at the Concert Hall

When it was announced that the world famous tenor Paulo Cuccinelli would be singing some arias at the concert hall, Joel and Julie decided to attend. They had <u>false perceptions</u> of meeting and touching the superstar, so they bought front-row seats.

The usher who seated them <u>playfully made reference</u> to the fact that the star gave autographs out to his fans in the front. Joel and Julie were so excited they hardly listened to the quiet <u>performance at the beginning</u> that the orchestra was playing before the appearance of the singer.

Finally Cuccinelli came out in a white tuxedo and the audience went wild before quieting down to hear him sing his favorite opera highlights. During the orchestra's <u>performance between the parts of the show</u>, many people tried to go backstage to see the famous tenor. A concert hall employee <u>misled them from the truth</u> by making them think that the star would sign autographs at the end of the show.

However, when the end came, Cuccinelli, being very <u>tending to sneak by</u>, <u>deceived and escaped</u> all the photographers and adoring public and disappeared into the evening. <u>With their deceptions taken away</u>, Joel and Julie returned home without an autograph of the star.

<u>Fill in the blanks using words from the **lud, lude, lus** family.</u>

1. Joel and Julie had _____ about getting close to the superstar tenor.

2. An usher _____ to the fact that the star gave autographs to front-row fans.

3. Their excitement made them miss the _____ played at the start of the show.

4. The orchestra performed an _____ during intermission.

5. In order to settle the fans down, an employee _____ them into believing that they could meet the star at the end of the show.

6. Cuccinelli was very _____ and no one got to see him at the end.

7. He even _____ the photographers and slipped away.

8. Joel and Julie, _____ back to reality, returned home.

Word Bank

alluded	deluded	eluded	illusions
alluding	disillusioned	elusive	interlude
alludingly	disillusioning	elusively	prelude

www.dynamicliteracy.com

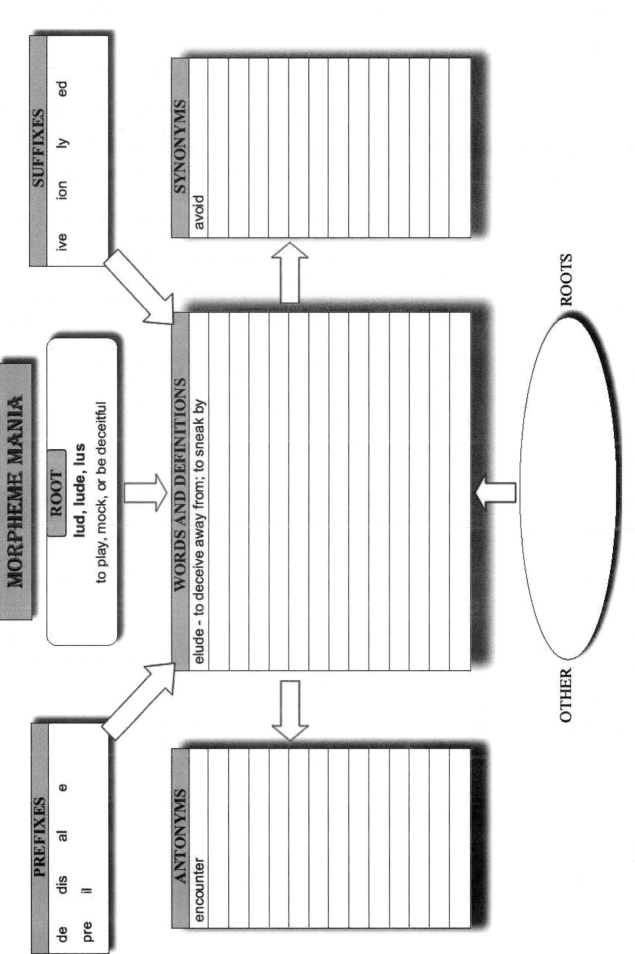

MORPHEME MANIA

PREFIXES
de	al	e
pre	il	

SUFFIXES
ive	ion	ly	ed

ROOT
lud, lude, lus
to play, mock, or be deceitful

WORDS AND DEFINITIONS
elude – to deceive away from; to sneak by

SYNONYMS
avoid

ANTONYMS
encounter

OTHER ROOTS

Build as many words as you can for this root family. Use the prefixes and suffixes listed, or add your own. If you use any "combining roots", add them to the "Other Roots" box. Try to think of an antonym and a synonym for each word you build.

www.DynamicLiteracy.com

Root: *lud, lude, lus*

Word	Synonym / Antonym	Word	Synonym / Antonym

Morphemes for this meaning family

Prefixes	Roots	Suffixes

Root Squares

How many words can you make?

Start in any square. Your goal is to combine two or more word parts to make as many words in the 'labor' family as you can. Write each word and a definition you can think of for it in the space provided at the bottom of the page.

s	col	ious
e	labor	or
ive	ory	ate

_____

_____

_____

_____

_____

_____

_____

_____

Magic Squares

Select the best answer for each of the words in the 'labor' family from the numbered definitions. Put the number in the proper space in the Magic Square box. If the total of the numbers is the same both across and down, you have found the magic number!

'labor' means work

WORDS	DEFINITIONS
A. collaborate	1. rooms equipped for work; scientific or medical workspaces
B. collaboration	2. worked together; acted as a team
C. elaborated	3. a room equipped for work; scientific or medical workspace
D. elaborately	4. people who work
E. laboratories	5. worked out; specified and explained in detail
F. laboriously	6. in a manner working together; so as to be done as teamwork
G. collaboratively	7. to work together; to act as a team
H. elaboration	8. in a manner worked out; in a manner specifying and explaining in detail
I. laborers	9. the act of working together; teamwork
	10. working
	11. the act of working out; act of specifying and explaining in detail
	12. in a manner full of work; strenuously

Magic Square Box

A.	B.	C.
D.	E.	F.
G.	H.	I.

Magic Number _____

www.dynamicliteracy.com

Stair Steps

Fill in the missing letters of each LABOR
word by using the definitions below.
LABOR means work

1.	l	a	b	o	r									
2.	l	a	b	o	r									
3.	l	a	b	o	r									
4.	l	a	b	o	r									
5.	l	a	b	o	r									
6.		l	a	b	o	r								
7.			l	a	b	o	r							
8.			l	a	b	o	r							
9.			l	a	b	o	r							

1. worked
2. people who work
3. full of work; strenuous
4. a room equipped for work; scientific or medical workspace
5. in a manner full of work; strenuously
6. acts of working out; acts of specifying and explaining in detail
7. working together; acting as a team
8. acts of working together; acts of teamwork
9. in a manner working together; so as to be done as teamwork

Work, Work, Work

In <u>rooms equipped for work</u> all over the country, researchers are <u>working</u> to find new ways to make life healthier. With their <u>worked out,</u> up-to-date equipment, they are <u>working together</u> with each other in a race against time. They find that <u>the act of working together</u>, like all teamwork, is best. They carry on <u>in a manner marked by work</u> and frequently give the public an <u>act of explaining the work</u> of the details of their <u>works</u>. In the <u>workplace</u> where scientific <u>workers</u> have <u>worked together</u> most, success has been fastest.

<u>Fill in the blanks with words from the **labor** family.</u>

1. Many scientific advancements come out of _____ across the country.

2. Researchers are _____ to find clues about making life healthier.

3. Much of their modern equipment is very _____.

4. In areas where scientists are _____, results come more quickly.

5. The act of _____ is good in most jobs.

6. Not only the research itself, but also the writing about the research, are done _____.

7. At intervals, researchers give an _____ about their _____.

8. The _____ encouraging the most teamwork among its _____ is usually the most successful.

9. Where people have _____, success has been fastest.

<u>Word Bank</u>

collaborate	collaborative	laboratories	laborers
collaborated	elaborate	laboratory	laboring
collaborating	elaborates	laborer	laboriously
collaboration	elaboration	laborer	labors

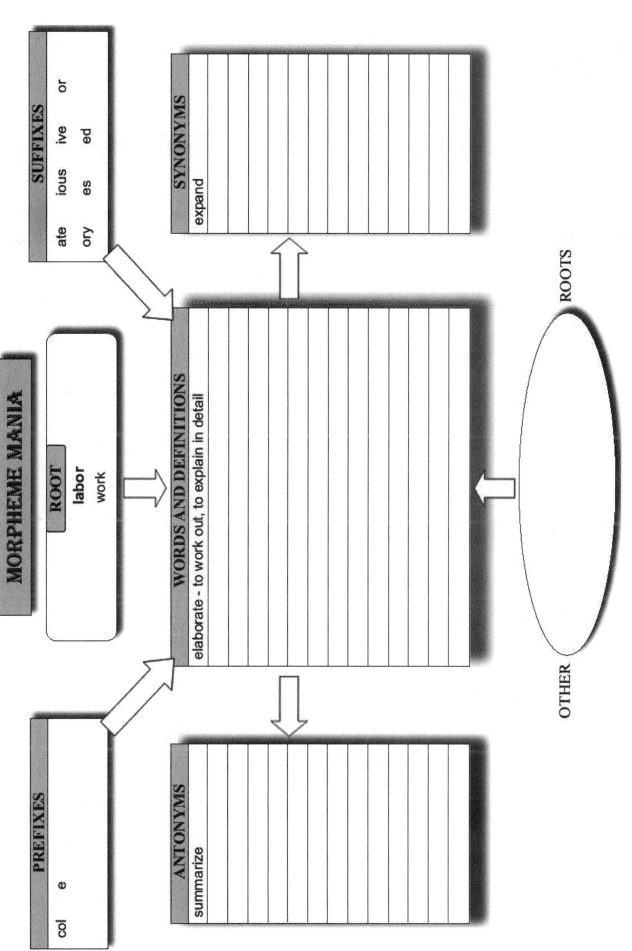

MORPHEME MANIA

PREFIXES

col e

ROOT

labor

work

SUFFIXES

ate ious ive or

ory es ed

WORDS AND DEFINITIONS

elaborate - to work out, to explain in detail

SYNONYMS

expand

ANTONYMS

summarize

ROOTS

OTHER

Build as many words as you can for this root family. Use the prefixes and suffixes listed, or add your own. If you use any "combining roots", add them to the "Other Roots" box. Try to think of an antonym and a synonym for each word you build.

www.DynamicLiteracy.com

Root: *labor*

Word	Synonym / Antonym	Word	Synonym / Antonym

Morphemes for this meaning family

Prefixes	Roots	Suffixes

www.dynamicliteracy.com

Suffixes

Suffix	Meaning
a (noun)	noun marker
a, ia (noun)	more than one
able, ab, abl, abil (adj)	having the power
ac (adjective)	related to
acle, acl, acul (noun)	result, means
acy, aci (noun)	act, process, quality
ade, ad (noun)	action, product
ade, ad (verb)	action
age, ag (noun)	result, place, action
age, ag (verb)	to do
al, all, ale, le (noun)	action, process
al, ial, ual (adjective)	characterized by
an (noun)	one belonging to or skilled in
anc, ance (noun)	action, process
ant (adjective)	performing
ant (noun)	thing or person doing
ar (adjective)	like; of or belonging to
ary, ari (adjective)	relating to
ary, ari (noun)	place; thing or person connected with
ate, at (noun)	office, function
ate, at, att (adjective)	acted upon, caused to be like
ate, at, att (verb)	to cause to become
cle, cl (noun)	little one
e, ue (noun)	noun marker
ed (adjective)	having been or made to become, characterized by
ed (verb)	did
ee (noun)	recipient or beneficiary of an action
el (noun)	small one
eme, em (noun)	unit, structure
ent, enc (adjective)	doing, behaving
ent, enc, ence (noun)	quality or state
er (adjective)	comparative form marker
er (noun)	person or thing that does
ery, eri, ry, ri (noun)	thing or place belonging to or connected with
est (adjective)	superlative marker
etic (adjective)	like, belonging to
ety, eti, et (noun)	state or quality or degree of
ful (adjective)	full of; characterized by
fy, fi (verb)	to make; to form into
i (noun)	plural marker
ia (noun)	condition, state
ian (noun)	person skilled in
iary, iari (adjective)	relating to
iary, iari (noun)	thing or place belonging to or connected with
iate, iat (verb)	to cause to become
ible, ib, ibil (adj)	capable, worthy
ic (adjective)	like, belonging to
ic (noun)	person or thing characterized by
ice (noun)	act, quality, condition
id (adjective)	resembling

Suffix	Meaning
id (noun)	one of a group
ify, ifi, if (verb)	to make; to form into
ile, ili, il (adjective)	capable of
ile, ili, il (noun)	part of
ing (adjective)	ongoing; in progress
ing (verb)	going on; happening
ion (noun)	result or outcome of an action or process
ious, eous (adjective)	full of; having; possessing qualities of
is (noun)	quality, condition, state
ish (verb)	to cause to become
isk (noun)	something having the shape of
ism (noun)	act or practice
ist (noun)	a person that performs an action
ite, it (adjective)	of, related to, suited for
ite, it (noun)	a native or product of
ite, it (verb)	to cause to become
ity, iti, it (noun)	state, quality, or degree of
ium (noun)	chemical, mass
ive, iv (adjective)	inclined to be or serving to
ive, iv (noun)	that which performs or serves to
ize, iz, ise, is (verb)	to cause to be like
less (adjective)	without, not having
ly (adjective)	like in appearance, manner, or nature
ly (adv)	in the manner of or so as to be
men, ment (noun)	result, process, act, condition
ness (noun)	state, condition, quality, degree
o (noun)	anything associated with
oid (noun)	something resembling
on, one (noun)	basic unit
or (noun)	a person or device that does; condition or activity
ory, ori (adjective)	of or relating to; serving for
ory, ori (noun)	something that relates to or is used for
ose, os, ous (adjective)	full of
otic (adjective)	of, related to, characterized by
s (noun)	designating a feature or activity
s, es (noun)	plural marker
s, es (verb)	he, she, or it does
sis (noun)	action or process
ty, ti, t (noun)	quality, condition, degree
uate, uat (verb)	to cause to become
uity, uiti, uit (noun)	state, quality, or degree of
ule, ul (noun)	small one
um (noun)	object or thing
uous, uos (adjective)	full of; having; possessing qualities of
ure, ur (noun)	act of, process, function
ure, ur (verb)	to do, to cause
us (noun)	act, result
y, i (noun)	state, condition, activity
y, i, ey (adjective)	characterized by, full of

WordBuild Elements Level 3 Index by Root

Root	Meaning	Page
form	shape, appearance, or arrangement	3
pon, pone, pos, pose, post	to place, to put	9
voc, voci, vok, voke	speech; voice, call, say	15
grat, grate, grati, grac, grace	agreeable, thankful, pleasing	21
gest	to take, bring, or carry	27
soci, socio	related to others-- companions, partners, allies	33
arch, archaeo, archa, arche, archi	early, chief, first, rule	39
ped, pede, pedi, pedo	foot; leg	45
nounc, nounce, nunci	report, message; say, speak	51
clud, clude, clus, cluse	to shut	57
it	to go; travel; passage	63
pot, pos, poss	powerful, able	69
merg, merge, mers, merse	to sink into or beneath the surface	75
mand, mend	to order; to put into someone's hand; entrust to	81
rupt	to break	87
cur, curr, curs	to run	93
fess, fant, fanti	to speak	99
phon, phone, phono	sound	105
art, arti, ert	skill, craft; joint; connected	111
sum, sume, sumpt	to take up, claim	117
tang, tag, ting, tig, tact	to touch, feel, perceive	123
bio, b, bi, be	life	129
nomin, nomen, nom, nomo	name	135
ordin, ord	row, rank, arrangement	141
centr, center, centri	center, middle, ordinary	147
cycl, cycle, cyclo	circle or wheel	153
migr	to move	159
don, done, dat, date	to give	165
cid, cide, cis, cise	to cut; kill or cut down	171
grav, grave, gravi, griev, grieve, grief	heavy or weight	177
viv, vive, vivi, vit	alive, life	183
sequ, secu, secut, secute	to follow	189
greg	flock, group	195
sacr, sacra, sacri, sacro, secr	holy, revered	201
lud, lude, lus	to play, mock, or be deceitful	207
labor	work, labor	213